MW00612765

Hidden History

of

CHATTANOOGA

Hidden History
of
CHATTANOOGA

Alexandra Walker Clark

THE
History
PRESS

Published by The History Press
Charleston, SC 29403
www.historypress.net

Cover and all contemporary photographs by Syrie Moskowitz unless otherwise noted.
Bottom cover photo by Will H. Stokes, courtesy of the Chattanooga Regional
History Museum.

First published 2008
Second printing 2012
Third printing 2013

ISBN 978-1-5402-1876-6

Library of Congress Cataloging-in-Publication Data

Clark, Alexandra Walker.
Hidden history of Chattanooga / Alexandra Walker Clark.
p. cm.
Includes bibliographical references.
ISBN 978-1-5402-1876-6
1. Chattanooga (Tenn.)--History. 2. Chattanooga (Tenn.)--Biography. I. Title.
F444.C457C58 2008
976.8'82--dc22
2008032138

Notice: The information in this book is true and complete to the best of our knowledge. It
is offered without guarantee on the part of the author or The History Press. The author
and The History Press disclaim all liability in connection with the use of this book.

This book is dedicated to the memory of:

Robert Sparks Walker
and
Wendell Clark Walker

With special thanks to:

Becky Eaves, Shirley Lawrence, Bess Neil, Cleata Wade Townsend, Peggy Hall, Tory Johnston, Joy Effron Adams and Tom Bibler

CONTENTS

Preface   9

Ross's Landing   11
Bluff View and Battery Place   15
University of Tennessee at Chattanooga
    and the Fort Wood District   23
Bottlers, Bakers and Burgers   29
African Americans in Early Chattanooga   33
The Firemen's Memorial Fountain   41
The Jewish Community in Early Chattanooga   43
Adolph Ochs: A Man of the Times   47
The Loss of Citico Mound   49
Grace Moore: Tennessee's Incomparable Songbird   53
Dragging Canoe: Fiercest Warrior of the Cherokee   57
A Castle in the Clouds   61
Almost Lost—Brainerd Mission   67
Audubon Acres: The Triumph of Robert Sparks Walker   75
Chickamauga Battlefield and Fort Oglethorpe   87
Once Upon a River: A Race to Preserve the Past   95
John David Gray and Graysville, Georgia   101
Blythewood Farms and the Hair Conrad Cabin   105
The Trail of Tears in the Chattanooga Area   111
The Grave of Nancy Ward, Beloved Woman
    of the Cherokee   123

Bibliography   127

PREFACE

Chattanooga, like the whole of our nation, is exceptional and multicultural, and its historic diversity makes the city particularly unique. The Chattanooga area is not simply the expression of one people, but a sum of the life and experience of all who have passed through time to walk this earth before us, in this particular place that is today called Chattanooga.

The successes and failures of our predecessors in this place—their triumphs and tragedies, their dreams and hard work—are their legacy to us, and greatly enrich the present. It is fitting to understand and appreciate these past efforts, even as we labor today to leave behind our own contribution for future generations.

To simplify the viewing of certain sites described in these pages, this book has been loosely organized by driving distances from downtown Chattanooga. However, as a few of these early historic subjects may only be seen in the mind, they must be created by the readers' imaginations, the originals having vanished long ago.

It is hoped that this book may contribute to a greater understanding of today's Chattanooga, viewed through the distant light of what has come before and helped to shape the present.

All photographs, unless otherwise noted, are by Syrie Moskowitz, whose internationally recognized work has appeared in exhibitions, galleries and publications around the world, and whose images may be viewed at www.syriekovitz.com.

ROSS'S LANDING

In town.

Long before present-day Chattanooga became part of Cherokee land, the Tennessee River, carving its serpentine route between Lookout and Signal Mountains, had already created an excellent natural port. In its 750-mile-long journey to join the Ohio River at Paducah, Kentucky, the great river's meanderings formed a seven-mile-long bend as it flowed past Chattanooga.

Once a part of Creek Indian land, the area had become a recognized part of the Cherokee lands by the early nineteenth century, when Scotsman Daniel Ross established his trading post where downtown Chattanooga proudly rises today.

Recognizing the business opportunities afforded by the site, Daniel Ross's son, John, and John's partner, Timothy Meigs, expanded the elder Ross's business, and built a landing and ferry there in 1815. John Ross also constructed a warehouse, and engaged in brisk commerce from this location, where boat cargoes were unloaded and driven by wagon to stores throughout the Cherokee Nation. With the death of Meigs in 1817, John Ross's brother Lewis became his partner in the thriving enterprises.

This growing trading center was known as Ross's Landing, but it was fated to take an active role in the Cherokee Removal. The landing was to become one of the points of departure for some two thousand reluctant Cherokees, who were imprisoned in an internment camp near the landing as they awaited removal.

These unfortunates were eventually forced at bayonet point into boats, and in June of 1838, the first three government-led detachments of Cherokees departed from Ross's Landing by flatboat. These three detachments would suffer deprivation and considerable loss of life, prompting the Cherokee leadership to obtain permission from the Federal government to supervise the remaining detachments of emigrating Cherokees without military intervention. John Ross, who had become Chief of the Cherokee Nation, would be the overseer of this tragic project.

The site of Ross's Landing is now submerged beneath the waters of Nickajack Lake, and located between Walnut and Market Street Bridges. But today a waterfront walkway known as the River Walk brings pedestrians alongside the waters of the Tennessee (the Cherokees' "Long Man") to a historic marker indicating the location of the former landing.

Contemporary Native American art honors the original residents of Chattanooga, and connects the city's downtown to the site of Ross's Landing.

Traditional Cherokee stickball players leap across the west wall of *The Passage* in downtown Chattanooga. The figures are part of an art installation designed by *Gadugi*, a group of five western Cherokee artists.

Serpentine stairway
leading up from the
River Walk to the
Hunter Art Museum.

The Passage is an installation created by five Oklahoma Cherokee artists, calling themselves *Gadugi*, a Cherokee word for "working together."

Figures of stickball players are represented on the north wall of *The Passage*, which is the largest public installation of southeastern Native American art. The west wall of *The Passage* features large ceramic medallions ornamented with symbols from Cherokee art, with both English and Cherokee syllabary text to interpret their meanings. A series of steps, partially covered in flowing water, lead up from the river to the remarkable Tennessee Aquarium, dedicated to freshwater aquatic life.

At the corner of Chestnut and Riverfront Streets stands the bronze sculpture of a Cherokee warrior by Jud Hartmann, honoring the people to whom this land once belonged prior to the arrival of the white man.

For years a blighted urban area, in a city once named as the nation's most polluted, the vibrant, pristine riverfront of today's Chattanooga teems

The imposing statue of a bronze Cherokee warrior by artist Jud Hartmann guards the corner of Chestnut and Riverfront Streets.

with tourist points of interest, restaurants, shops and wonderfully whimsical art. Among the unexpected sculptures around Market Street are a water mill by artist Terry West and a curving, overstuffed sofa, both masterfully constructed of brick. Multiple fountains spray enticing jets of crystalline waters, while otters, turtles and other freshwater denizens await within the imposing Tennessee Aquarium, to the delight of children and adults alike.

Encircling this beating heart of civilization, Chattanooga's ancient mountains and river remain, silent witnesses to the rise and fall of more than one culture. Like the distant mountain in *The Course of Empire*, Thomas Cole's classic series of five allegorical paintings depicting the permanence of nature and transience of man and his civilization, they keep the record of our time as stewards of our planet earth, and how we have chosen to care for it.

BLUFF VIEW AND
BATTERY PLACE

In town.

Although little remains visible today of its past involvement with industry, in 1854, the now-picturesque Bluff View was the site of a pig iron–producing blast furnace with a forty-foot-high stack, the operation known as Bluff Furnace. Built by two ironmasters, Robert Cravens and James Whiteside, the plant successfully produced pig iron until 1860, when a shortage of coke forced it to shut down. As the Civil War loomed, most of its equipment was transported to Alabama. During the Federal occupation of Chattanooga, Union troops used its furnace stack as a lime kiln, but would ultimately tear down all the furnace's remaining structures. It has been suggested that the hewn limestone blocks from Bluff Furnace may have been used in the 1890 construction of the massive stone footings of Walnut Street Bridge.

A model of Bluff Furnace is a reminder of its former presence, and a 1981 excavation of the site revealed significant archaeological data. A detailed documentation of its history is presented in the book, *Industry and Technology in Antebellum Tennessee*, written by Council, Honerkamp and Will.

In 1862, Chattanooga's Battery Place, located on a high point southeast of the Tennessee River, was the site of a crude military fort, housing cannons that rained destruction down on the river town below. Chattanooga would become a hotly contested prize during the Civil War. While the better-known battles for control of the city are the Battle Above the Clouds, the Battle of Missionary Ridge and the bloody Battle of Chickamauga, this prominent bluff above the river and its convenient port proved an admirable location for launching bombardment. Fortunately for the citizens beneath this hill, most of the shells fired down from this site, as well as from Lookout Mountain

A miniature replica of Robert Cravens's Bluff Furnace marks its site, overlooking the Tennessee River. The iron-producing blast furnace operated from 1854 to 1860.

and Missionary Ridge, were intended for use against advancing troops, and lacked the force to strike targets of any significant distance.

In 1940, Mrs. Walline, an elderly resident who had lived at 107 Battery Place since 1904, recalled to one local writer that by the early 1890s, all remains of the old fort's presence had been cleared away to give place for the development of residential building lots on the former military site. She also reported the reappearance of wild passionflowers, which had once grown rampant on the old fort's remains but that had been thought destroyed during the construction in the area in the 1900s. Walline's two-story home had once provided a grand view of the Tennessee River below, but by the 1960s, it and several blocks of Battery Place itself were torn down and the earth literally removed to make way for the new highway that now cuts through the area.

The Tennessee's magnificent, extending limestone bluffs rise some eighty feet above the river, and have proved irresistible to the human eye, giving rise to a number of grand estates that still cling to their precarious lots with the incomparable vista. So high and steep are these plunging bluffs that early residents of the place were often referred to as the "cliff dwellers."

One of the early bluff mansions was built in 1904 by insurance broker Ross Faxon. Its ownership was later transferred to the prominent Hunter family, and it has since become the home of the prestigious Hunter Art Museum. Opening in 1952, this acclaimed museum offers both permanent and changing exhibits from its spectacular location.

Bluff View and Battery Place

Icarus takes flight above the Tennessee River, from the Bluff View District's River Gallery Sculpture Garden. Dramatic, torch-welded sculpture by Russell Whiting.

The Bluff View area has long been a draw for visitors, and even as early as the first decade in the 1900s, its homes were considered a spot worthy of tourist attention. A hand-painted enamel souvenir spoon from this period—lettered "Bluff View, Chattanooga, Tenn."—depicts its towering wall of limestone rising from the river and many large, prominent homes collected across the rocky summit.

In proximity to the Hunter Art Gallery is Chattanooga's oldest existing structure, spanning the Tennessee River—the Walnut Street Bridge. Built in 1890, it was intended to connect downtown Chattanooga to neighborhoods on the river's north shore. Prior to its construction, a ferryboat provided access across the river. This vessel was quite slow, being propelled by a mule walking in a circle at the north end of Market Street. With the bridge's completion, the mule was removed from ferry duty and retired, at about the same time electricity liberated mules from towing the town's streetcars.

For decades, the narrow bridge from Walnut Street served its noble purpose, providing access long after subsequent bridges leading from downtown Chattanooga were built across the Tennessee. However, on several occasions over the years, the bridge fell into such disrepair that it was periodically shut down. When it was at last permanently closed to all vehicular traffic in 1978, there was speculation that the old landmark was slated to be demolished. Eventually, however, a $4 million restoration project began, and in 1991 the bridge again opened, for foot traffic only.

More than a century ago, in stark contrast to its present service to tourism, this bridge was twice the site of racial tragedy. On two separate occasions, in 1893 and again in 1906, enraged mobs succeeded in breaking into the city jail and removing two black prisoners who had been accused of raping white women. Both men were hanged from the bridge.

Local author Robert Sparks Walker, who kept a journal for more than sixty years until his death in 1960, recorded the following, regarding the 1906 incident:

> *I recently purchased a Stevens shotgun for use in hunting game with my brothers in the country. While snapping the hammer hunting geese, I broke a spring and took it to the Umbrella Shop for a new one. On my way home from work downtown at my paper, The Southern Fruit Grower, I paid for the repair, shouldered my gun and walked on home in the dark, stopping a moment at the Hamilton County Jail to say hello to folks I knew who worked there. Our house is about four blocks from the Walnut Street Bridge, and imagine my shock the next morning to see on the Times' front page, the horrible story of the lynching of Ed Johnson, a Negro.*
>
> *A mob had forced the jailer, an old man, to unlock Johnson's cell, and they took the unfortunate man to the bridge near my house and hanged him! He had been accused of picking up a white woman in St. Elmo and raping her in Forest Hills Cemetery. Besides the violent crimes involved, I was horrified to think I might have been arrested on circumstantial evidence as having taken part in that murderous mob! Anyone who saw me could have testified that I was in the vicinity of the jail, carrying a shotgun on my shoulder!*

These bleak events have taken their place in a troubled history, and today the fully restored Walnut Street Bridge is now a benign pedestrian walkway across the river. A half-mile in length, it is boasted to be the longest pedestrian bridge in the world, providing grand views of the Bluffs, Maclellan Island, the mountains and downtown Chattanooga.

On the north shore of the river, located in present-day Coolidge Park, one of the bridge's massive fifty-foot-high limestone block pylons serves as a wall climb for those whose interests lie in the pursuit of rock climbing. Operated by the Adventure Guild, the stone tower is open for climbing from April through November (call 423.266.5709 for information).

Bluff View and Battery Place

Outdoor adventures include scaling one of the Walnut Street Bridge limestone footings.

Another former dwelling in the Bluff View area, situated at 712 High Street, is now the Houston Museum, housing antiques and decorative arts. Located in an 1892 brick Victorian building, and open year-round, the museum is home to an astonishing collection of early art glass and fine china, all assembled by a most unlikely collector, Anna Safley Houston, locally known as "Antique Annie."

An eccentric and somewhat mysterious antique dealer who also boasted a double-digit collection of husbands, Anna was considered a local character during her lifetime. Fellow streetcar riders would often report home with amusement that they had been present when she climbed aboard with a peculiar lamp or oversized pitcher secured under her arm. But although she lived in virtual poverty for the last decade and a half of her life—sleeping on the floor until her death from malnutrition in 1951 at age seventy-five—she possessed extraordinary vision and an appreciation for finer things. When she left all her treasures to the City of Chattanooga, Houston became the unexpected benefactress to a city that did not yet understand her importance. But these honors would come with time. Today, her collections have literally been valued as priceless, worth uncalculated millions, and are famous worldwide.

Just around the corner from Annie's museum are still more elegant former homes of Bluff View. Although once a prestigious residential area, today these dwellings above the river, housing a variety of businesses and restaurants, have become recognized as an important arts community.

Victorian brick home at 712 High Street is now the Annie Houston Museum, and houses her extensive collection of rare glass and china.

A stroll down East Second Street brings the visitor to the first of the three Bluff View Inns. A striking English Tudor building built in 1889, Maclellan House is the former residence of the R.J. Maclellan family, tenaciously perched on the upper north side of the street. Maclellan House offers six guest rooms, and from its backyard and windows is seen a magnificent view of the river and Maclellan Island below. Many of the inn's elegant furnishings, including a remarkable Victorian square grand piano with mother-of-pearl keys and inlay, are original to the home.

Maclellan Island, approximately twenty acres in size, was first known as Ross's Landing Island, and later Chattanooga Island. Once reputed to be a refuge for runaway slaves, and later the haunt of vagrants, it was purchased by the Maclellans and other early Bluff View residents, who wished to protect its property and their view. Now a wildlife preserve, the island was donated to the local Audubon Society in 1954 by Coca-Cola magnate R.J. Maclellan, and renamed Maclellan Island in his honor.

Today this property is accessible by boat, and the two-mile hiking trail around the island's perimeter provides glimpses of its diversity of plant and animal life—among them a blue heron rookery at the island's upstream tip. There are also nesting waterfowl, mink, muskrat, beaver, turtles, raccoons and fox—all most unlikely residents in the heart of a bustling city. An unusual

Rare, square grand piano with fretwork and mother-of-pearl inlay and keys stands in the front parlor of Bluff View Inn, and is original to the house.

Perched on the bluffs overlooking the Tennessee River, the Bluff View Inn was built in 1899, and was the home of R.J. Maclellan.

feature is a "rain shadow desert," caused by the crossing of Veterans Bridge over the downstream third of the island. Excursions to Maclellan Island may be arranged through the Chattanooga Audubon Society.

Back on the bluff, the second home comprising the Bluff View Inns is the stately Martin House at 412 East Second, a brick Colonial Revival home built in 1927 across the street from Maclellan House. It presents a wide veranda with views of the Tennessee River and offers three guest rooms upstairs. Its first floor is now the elegant Back Inn Café, offering fine world cuisine. Additionally, a third former residence, Thompson House, built in 1908 and located around the corner at 212 High Street, features several guest rooms, two suites and a front porch facing the mountains for sunset views.

The successful transformation from fading residential neighborhood to Bluff View's present arts community status is the result of the vision of Dr. and Mrs. Charles Portera. In 1992, they initiated the area's renaissance with the opening of the fine art and craft–oriented River Gallery, located in the French stucco house at 400 East Second Street, which was once the home of Dr. Edward Newell. One year later, River Gallery opened the River Gallery Sculpture Garden, situated at the end of Second Street, on a dramatic overlook of the Tennessee River.

Featuring more than thirty works of original sculpture by world-renowned artists such as H. Dan Jackson, Allan Houser, Richard Serra, Frank Stella, Russell Whiting, Tom Wesselman, Mary Lynn Portera, Leonard Baskin, Earnest Trova, Jim Collins, Isamu Noguchi and many others, this permanent outdoor exhibit is a powerfully dramatic combination of natural and man-made beauty, and not to be missed.

The Bluff View Art District occupies only one and a half city blocks, but within this vital space thrive Rembrandt's Coffee House and Roasting Company, the Renaissance Commons conference center, Bluff View Bakery, a bocce ball court and terrace, Tony's Pasta Shop and Trattoria, the Back Inn Café and the Chocolate Kitchen.

Dedicated to architectural preservation, beautiful landscaping and the culinary, as well as the visual, arts, the Porteras' dream of revitalizing this all-but-forgotten neighborhood has become a joyous reality—a treasure of a gift to the reemerging city.

UNIVERSITY OF TENNESSEE AT CHATTANOOGA AND THE FORT WOOD DISTRICT

McCallie Avenue, in town.

Founded in 1886 as Chattanooga University, the school merged in 1889 with the U.S. Grant University at Athens, Tennessee, thus forming two campuses of Grant University—one in Athens, and one in Chattanooga. Initially a Methodist-based institution, Grant University's early presidents were Methodist ministers.

In 1907, the Chattanooga campus separated from Grant University to become the University of Chattanooga, until it merged with the University of Tennessee in 1969 and became the University of Tennessee at Chattanooga.

Although the campus has grown considerably through the years, many of its older buildings still exist, making it an attractive background for higher learning. A number of these are handsome examples of early twentieth-century architecture, some of which extend into the adjacent historic Fort Wood District.

Within the UTC campus, at 725 Oak Street, is the Cadek Conservatory of Music. Although the present building dates from the late 1960s, the conservatory was originally founded in 1904 by violinist and orchestra conductor Joseph Ottokar Cadek, a Bohemian immigrant.

By the time of his death in 1927, Jospeh Cadek's profound dedication to music and his community had developed a level of artistic achievement that was exceptional in his day. The Chattanooga Symphony Orchestra and the Chattanooga Opera have both emerged under the inspiring influence of the Cadek Conservatory. The conservatory became affiliated with the University of Chattanooga in 1953, and contributed largely to establishing its music department. In 1973, UTC became owners of the conservatory, which is now also the home of UTC's choral department and the WUTC radio station.

As UTC has developed and expanded over the years, newer and modern structures rub shoulders with the "old guard" of campus buildings. The original University Hall, built in 1886, stood four stories tall and sported a gilt tower. Known as "Old Main," the building became unstable, and was torn down in 1917, but its former site now forms the center of the campus quadrangle. Three historic buildings face into the quadrangle: Founders Hall, built around 1916, which houses the chancellor's office and others; Hooper-Race Hall, built in 1916, now the center for records and registration; and Patten Chapel, built in 1919 by Dr. John Patten, Patten's daughter being the first to be married there.

The chapel has since become a location for important ceremonies and so popular among prospective brides that it is rumored to have a two-year waiting list. Campus lore says there are even some young ladies who have signed the list to hold future nuptials under its roof, with the space for the intended groom left blank.

Fletcher Hall, built in 1939 and located on the corner of McCallie Avenue and Douglas Street, was once the Chattanooga City Library until 1974, housing both the local and university collections. It is now the business office and political science department.

The handsome brick building at the corner of Douglas and Oak Streets, built in 1910, was formerly the chancellor's home. Today it houses the development offices, focusing on fundraising.

Several of the university's earlier structures face the designated pedestrian-only part of Oak Street. South Stadium, across from the Hooper-Race Hall, was built in 1908. It is slated to undergo renovations and become the future alumni house. Next door to South Stadium is Bretske Hall; formerly the campus cafeteria until 1970, it now houses the geoscience department.

At the corner of Oak and Palmetto Streets, within the Fort Wood District but also on campus, stands the Z.C. Patten House, built in 1892 by the founder of Chattanooga Medicine Company. The brick Italianate house was designed by Samuel Patton, one of Chattanooga's significant architects, and is presently home to the Alumni Affairs Department. Two Civil War cannons occupy its front lawn, signifying its former location as a military fortification site. Further exploration down Oak Street reveals some handsome examples of Queen Anne, Tudor and Classical Revival architecture.

Set on a hill, the Fort Wood District was named for a Civil War earthen redoubt, built around 1863 by Union troops at the hill's crest. It was one of three such remaining reminders of the war, until it succumbed to land development in the 1880s. Originally named Fort Creighton, for Colonel William Creighton, it was soon after renamed in honor of General Thomas Wood.

Today it is the setting for a picturesque neighborhood filled with exceptional homes, reflecting late Victorian and Classical Revival architecture. Many of Chattanooga's prominent families built elegant residences in this area, which remained a fashionable neighborhood until the mid-1950s, when it began to experience a decline.

In recent years, a resurgence of energy and restoration has begun, making Fort Wood once more a beautiful and desirable neighborhood. New families have moved in and teamed with older residents to form the Fort Wood Community Association, which is active in revitalizing the area, having placed some 120 local structures on the National Registry of Historic Places. Many, though not all, of these handsome, historic homes feature markers on the sidewalk that designate their history, making it worth taking a walking or driving tour through the neighborhood to appreciate.

Located at 801 Vine Street, on the corner of Palmetto Street, is the thirteen-thousand-square-feet Romanesque limestone Mayor's Mansion Inn, which was built in 1889 and originally known as the Watkins House. Edmond Watkins served as mayor of Chattanooga from 1897 to 1899. Reservations and tours of the property are available by appointment. (For information, call 423.265.5000.) The 800 block of Vine Street also includes such gems as the exotic Warner House, built in 1891 by Major Joseph Warner, and the William MacAdoo House, built in 1888.

Highlighting the 900 block of Vine are the Kosmos Women's Club, built in 1910; the T. Olmstead House, built in 1904; the Senter School House, built in 1904; and Fort Wood Apartments, built in 1928, which offered such innovations as built-in refrigerators and bedroom jewelry vaults. Also in this block are the Kappa Sigma Fraternity House, built in 1905, and the J. Conn Guild House, built in 1899, which in 1902 became the residence of Guild, who designed Incline no. 2 up Lookout Mountain.

The Colonial Revival building at 508 Fort Wood Place was built in 1915 by George F. Milton, president of the Chattanooga News Company. Following his death in 1924, his widow, Abby Crawford Milton, avidly pursued her interests in political activism and literature. She was heavily involved with the Chattanooga branch of the woman's suffrage movement.

Although she held a degree from the Chattanooga College of Law, she never practiced law, instead using her degree as a credential in her work to bring about ratification of the Nineteenth Amendment, granting women the right to vote. She was active in establishing the Great Smoky Mountains

National Park, and supported the Tennessee Valley Authority (TVA) during its inception.

Milton wrote poetry, and also compiled a collection of poems, *Strains From a Dulcimore*, by an earlier Chattanooga poet and naturalist, Emma Bell Miles. Milton's own books of poetry include *Caesar's Wife and Other Poems*, *Flower Lore*, *Grandma Says* and *The Magic Switch*.

Milton and author/naturalist Robert Sparks Walker became close friends a few years after her husband's passing. Their interests in literature and the natural world brought them together, and they spent many afternoons working outdoors, critiquing poetry projects.

In September 1929, Walker wrote: "Mrs. Milton and I are working on getting published a book of poems written by the late Tennessee poet, Emma Bell Miles. Abby has a scrapbook containing many of them, and I hope I may be of some assistance to her in this. She [Miles] and Mrs. Milton were good friends, she often visiting in Mrs. Milton's home."

In October of the same year, he continues: "We discussed plans to bring out a book of Miles' poems, and then drove to the homeplace of Chief John Ross, which is presently operated as a chicken dinner restaurant and miniature golf course by Mrs. Robert Cooke."

The widowed Milton and widower Walker continued their friendship born of mutual interests, and in a June, 1930 entry in Walker's journal, he comments:

> *I have seen much these past months of Mrs. Milton, who either sends over her chauffeur or picks me up herself. We have begun the pleasant practice of parking in a scenic field or woods, to work on manuscripts. I like working outdoors so much that we may continue this, in spite of speculations that may rise from it. She has invited me for dinner several times, and I always enjoy her company. We have at last succeeded in placing the Miles' book of verse, "Strains From a Dulcimore," with Bozart Press.*
>
> *I am glad we have the use of each other's ears for criticism, for when I tried to get [son] Wendell's and [niece] Dona's attention, I had to first tie them to the cookstove while I read to them. But they have mutinied, extracting my promise to grant them future immunity from any such verbal torture.*

In 1942, Walker revisited his former affiliations with both Miles and Milton:

I again reflected on my past friendship with Mrs. Milton, and how I wrote letter upon letter in her behalf to find this volume, ("Strains From a Dulcimore"), a publisher. Mrs. Miles was a gifted naturalist and writer, but she married a native mountaineer who could never earn sufficient income to provide for his family. His wife supplemented their income by the sale of paintings and writings, but even so, from my brief acquaintance with her and her four children, I think she knew much joy from the elements in nature with which she was so well acquainted.

[Miles's] first book went into only one edition. Her second book on birds, at the time I wound up her estate as her administrator [in 1919], had not earned sufficient royalties to pay her funeral expenses, even though at that time two thousand copies had sold. In her posthumously published book of poems, which Mrs. Milton edited, I wrote lines in the preface comparing her to the birds and wildflowers she loved so well. There was much of the mystical woodthrush in this woman [Miles].

The Milton home on Fort Wood Place was, for a time, a bed-and-breakfast, but is now once more a private residence and not open to the public. Abby Crawford Milton, poet and pioneer champion of women's rights, died at the age of 110 in 1991.

BOTTLERS, BAKERS
AND BURGERS

In town.

Most people have grown up eating fast food. Americans like their sodas, burgers and sweets, and Chattanoogans are no exception. The residents of Chattanooga are literally surrounded by fast food history, the success of these local treats indicative of their long-running appreciation.

Coca-Cola has its roots in the South, having been created in Atlanta, Georgia, in 1886 by a pharmacist, Dr. John Pemberton, whose interest was the creation of medicinal syrups. He was soon selling the beverage mixed with soda water to a local pharmacy.

As the drink gained in popularity, two Chattanooga businessmen, Benjamin Thomas and Joseph Whitehead, sought out the product's current Atlanta owner with the intention of securing the bottling rights. After much persuasion, they were able to obtain their goal, and together with a third partner, John T. Lupton, they opened with world's first Coca-Cola Bottling Company in 1899.

The venture was an overwhelming success, and by 1909 there were almost four hundred Coca-Cola bottling plants in operation in the country. The original Chattanooga plant was located at 17 Market Street, where Patten Parkway is today; after relocating once, the company moved in 1970 to its present site at 4000 Amnicola Highway.

The original "Coke" bottle was the Hutchinson, which used a stoppered cap. It was replaced by a straight-sided bottle with a diamond shaped paper label, and the logo embossed on the neck. The first curved-shape design came out in 1916, and was known as the Hobbleskirt, or contour bottle, much like the ones so easily recognized today.

Nothing is more iconic of Southern fast food than a "Coke," served up with that well-known and beloved foodstuff of childhood, the chocolate and marshmallow treat—the Moon Pie.

The Chattanooga Bakery was founded in the early 1900s as an offshoot of the Mountain City Flour Mill. The Hutcheson family, the mill's owners, made the decision to use the mill's surplus flour by opening a bakery on King Street. The bakery's success soon began to rival that of its parent flour mill, and by 1910, its ovens were producing more than two hundred baked treats, such as Butterette Dainties, Mace Jumbles, Peek-a-Boo Iced Cookies, Peanuckle, Jersey Cream Lunch Biscuits and the Buster.

In addition to these, and marketed under the bakery's own Lookout Brand, honoring the city's landmark mountain, were Raisin Cookies, Graham Sandwiches, Salty Crackers, Lemon Drop Cakes and Lookout Sugar Cookies, to name but a few. Yet a still greater invention was to come, one that would catapult the Chattanooga Bakery into national consciousness.

Yes—it was that decadent Moon Pie! This creation was the collective brainchild of the bakery's employees. With a flavor reminiscent of the ultimate campers' feast, the s'more (a dripping, gummy compilation of melted chocolate bar sections and gluey marshmallows, all stuck precariously to a graham cracker over a blazing campfire, to be eaten with the utmost care and several napkins), the Moon Pie is by comparison a deliciously sophisticated and pristine dessert food.

It is best described as a round, graham cookie sandwich with marshmallow filling, the whole of which is entirely dipped in chocolate. It was introduced in 1917, reportedly by a company salesman, in the interest of fulfilling mining customers' requests for a tasty but handy dessert that could be packed in a lunch pail. As a result, Moon Pies have now been filling lunch boxes for over ninety years.

The Chattanooga Bakery has relocated to 900 Manufacturers Road, and is presently studying the feasibility of offering tours of its premises, to show the making of this historic treat. More information is available on their website, http://www.moonpie.com/history.asp.

Yet another first in fast food was established in Chattanooga during the Great Depression, and its enduring popularity has made it the second oldest fast food chain in America. The first Krystal opened its doors in 1932 at Seventh and Cherry Streets in downtown Chattanooga, and although the original building still stands, it is no longer a hamburger restaurant. However, the enterprise not only survived its unlikely timing, it has developed into a thriving business today.

Bottlers, Bakers and Burgers

Krystal was founded by Rody B. Davenport Jr., whose background was textiles, and his partner, J.G. Sherrill, who were much impressed by the success of a Northern-based hamburgers business, White Castle. For their Krystal venture, Davenport and Sherrill chose the distinctive spelling, which was to be indicative of the "crystal clean" environment in which the signature steamed, square, oniony hamburgers were sold for a nickel apiece. Who could resist such a deal? Chattanooga burger fans flocked to Krystal's doors, and they continue to do so, even though the price has risen moderately with the times.

As Krystal has expanded, it has remained predominately a Southeastern chain, Davenport having made an agreement with the "Yankee" White Castle early on, due to their similar product, not to cross the invisible Mason-Dixon line. This gentlemen's compact has not only spared the country a resurging Civil War fought in ketchup and hamburger meat, but has kept Krystal a particularly beloved Southern food icon, with Chattanooga as its heart.

AFRICAN AMERICANS IN EARLY CHATTANOOGA

In town.

After the Indian Removal in 1838, Ross's Landing was renamed Chattanooga, and began its expansion into a city. Its population would reach two thousand by the 1860s. Businesses began to spring up to accommodate the influx of new citizens that poured into the area—most of them whites, but also a quantity of slaves and freed blacks.

The Western and Atlantic Railway, built from 1837 to 1850 by English entrepreneur John Gray and his brother William, would travel from Atlanta, Georgia, and terminate in Chattanooga. Besides the immediate effects its completion had on the community at large, it was inadvertently destined to make Chattanooga famous almost a century later for the 1940s hit song, "Chattanooga Choo-Choo."

Industry joined with this improved transportation in 1854, when Robert Cravens constructed his ambitious Bluff Furnace on the cliffs above the Tennessee River downtown. But Chattanooga's emergence into the nineteenth-century fast lane of commerce, as well as its prime river location, served to make it a significant target for both the North and the South during the Civil War.

No one man may have more appreciated the tenuous condition of the Chattanooga citizen in those trying days of civil turmoil than William "Uncle Bill" Lewis. Born a slave in Winchester, Tennessee, Lewis came to Chattanooga in 1837, prior to the Removal. There he succeeded in establishing a successful blacksmithing shop at the corner of Seventh and Market Streets. From its revenues, he was able to purchase both his and his wife's freedom, and in 1851, that of his mother, brother and sister.

But Lewis, who could not have had much sympathy for the occupying Confederates, was in 1862 given the undesirable task of forging the leg irons for the Union spies known as Andrews' Raiders.

At Kennesaw, Georgia, Andrews and his five men boldly boarded a Western and Atlantic train named the *General*, planning to head north with the engine while burning railroad bridges and destroying the rails behind them. Had this plan succeeded, it would have cut off supplies to the South, and in theory, brought the war to an early close.

But when the *General* ran low on fuel near Graysville, the plan failed. Andrews and his men took to the woods, and were soon captured. Andrews's raiding party was fated to become the unwilling residents of Swaim's Jail in Chattanooga, in proximity to the home of William Lewis.

Confederate General Leadbetter, a man not known for his mercy, had ordered that four of the captured raiders be sent to "the hole," by which he meant the old slave jail situated on Lookout Street between Fourth and Fifth Streets on a hill at the east end of town. The jail was a fenced two-story brick building, operated by a man named John Swaim, some sixty years of age. A locking trapdoor in the floor of the main holding cell led down by a ladder some thirteen feet to "the hole," a rat-infested, overcrowded dungeon intended for runaway slaves.

Lewis, who raised lettuce and secretly sympathized with the raiders, obtained permission from their jailers to send some of his produce to the prisoners. Imagine Lewis's anguish following James Andrews's escape from his first imprisonment in "the hole," and subsequent recapture, when one of Lewis's workmen was obliged to visit the dungeon and attach a pair of heavy leg irons around Andrews's ankles to prevent him from escaping a second time.

The leader of the ill-fated raid was soon after hanged in Atlanta, and by the late twentieth century, the site of Swaim's Jail would become a parking lot. But William Lewis would continue to prosper, and sent a number of his children north to receive a good education.

The Civil War came full force to Chattanooga in 1863; the struggle for its control resulting in three now-famous and bloody conflicts known as the Battle of Chickamauga, the Battle of Missionary Ridge and the Battle of Lookout Mountain. The Union victory of November 25, 1863, ended Confederate control of the city.

On Christmas Day 1863, General George Thomas, "the Rock of Chickamauga," issued orders to create a national cemetery to commemorate the battles for Chattanooga. Thomas had already selected the site during the Battle of Missionary Ridge, in which his troops had been victorious.

African Americans in Early Chattanooga

Thomas's choice was a sloping hundred-foot-high hill, comprised of approximately seventy-five acres, facing Missionary Ridge on one side and Lookout Mountain on the other. The summit of this property, purchased from locals Joseph Ruohs, Robert Hooke and J.R. Slayton, had been General Grant's headquarters for four days during the Battle of Lookout Mountain.

As the land was cleared and developed, it became evident that a third of the site could not be used for burials due to its many limestone outcroppings. The dense oak forest formerly on the property had largely been felled during its occupation as a battleground. The introduction of replacement evergreens and flowering shrubs were then chosen to landscape the numerous burial sites. Plots for officers were laid out around a central monument, with the graves of enlisted men forming concentric circles around them. It was designated Chattanooga National Cemetery in 1867. By 1870, in contained over 12,800 burials—8,685 known and 4,189 unknown.

Following the September, 1862 issuance of the Emancipation Proclamation, official enrollment of both runaway slave and free African Americans began in the Union army. Over 178,000 African Americans, comprising 163 units, served in the Union army during the last two years of the Civil War, and even more African Americans served in the Union navy.

By August 1863, there were fourteen Negro regiments ready for service, their presence strengthening the Union during a most critical time. By war's end, the United States Colored Troops made up almost a tenth of the total number of Union troops.

In Chattanooga's National Cemetery, the letters "USCT," for United States Colored Troops, identify a number of African American Civil War soldiers' graves, and there are more that are unmarked on the back side of the cemetery.

In his 1939 journal, local writer Robert Sparks Walker recounts a latter, poignant event that took place in the cemetery:

> *Last August a Negro soldier who died in battle was buried in National Cemetery. Captain Henderson, superintendent of the place, told me the man's dog came in with mourners at the burial, entering by auto, but refusing to leave. No one could catch him, and he has since lived as a wild dog in a rock cave near the grave. He will have nothing to do with people, but remains, half-starved, guarding his master's grave...*
>
> *I have learned that the faithful dog who refused to leave the man's grave in the National Cemetery met his death last January in the zero weather. Despite cold, hunger and grief, the man's dog had kept watch over his beloved master until he froze to death on the spot. What loyalty!*

Perhaps the cave referred to might have been the one that can be seen as you drive through the back section of the cemetery. It was closed up long ago with hewn limestone, but as caves often do, it comes with an unproven rumor. During the Civil War, when Grant's headquarters occupied the hill, the cave and connecting tunnels beneath the cemetery were reportedly used to transport secret military messages. Although unconfirmed, the story is plausible, given Chattanooga's underground honeycombs of limestone.

The Chattanooga National Cemetery is located at 1200 Bailey Avenue in Chattanooga, Tennessee. An index of burials is available outside the cemetery office.

In the decades following the Civil War and the abolition of slavery, Chattanooga would become home to many more black citizens, who considered their safety more secure in larger cities, rather than in rural communities. In 1867, the racial divide was bridged by the First Congregationalist Church of Chattanooga, which became the first Southern church to accept both black and white members.

As the African American population increased, many sought to establish their businesses and practice their professions in Chattanooga. The roster of these early entrepreneurs is impressive. Daniel Hall established the Enterprise Manufacturing Company at 423 Chestnut Street; G.W. Turner came to Chattanooga in 1881 and became one of several grocers to open their own stores—his two stories, at the corner of Cowart and Montgomery Streets; and J.A. Strickland, who came to town in 1885 and became president of the Rising Sun Manufacturing Company at 1312 Harrison Street.

The first free public school for African Americans opened in 1875, at Seventh and Vine Streets. After a year in operation, it was taken over by the city school system. James A. Henry, Atlanta University graduate, became the first black principal of Chattanooga's Howard High School in 1884, holding the position until his death in 1914. Howard awarded its first high school diploma in 1886 to Bell Washington, who became a teacher.

J.M. Easterling arrived in 1887, and seven years later opened a tailor shop at 903 Georgia Avenue. John Drain, by 1888, had two barber shops. Charles Grigsby owned a merchandise store in 1888, and was elected to the city council in 1905. Journalist Randolph Miller started his own newspaper, the *Weekly Blade*, in 1898. And Thomas Wilson Hagler founded the Chattanooga National Medical College in 1899.

J.W. White, banker, in 1890 established the Chattanooga Penny Bank. George W. Franklin opened a funeral parlor in 1894 at 728 Chestnut Street. John Lovell, blacksmith and real estate investor, owned a large race horse farm, which is now Lovell Field Airport. Dr. O.L. Davis, a Chattanooga native from Lookout Mountain, was the first female dentist in town, with an office in the James Building on East Ninth Street.

By the turn of the twentieth century, there was a growing number of well-trained African American doctors in Chattanooga. One particularly remarkable physician, Dr. Emma R. Wheeler, a 1905 graduate of Walden University's Medical, Dental and Pharmaceutical College (only one of three women in her class), would establish Walden Hospital in 1915.

Using her own money, Wheeler purchased the property on the corner of East Eighth and Douglas Streets, where she built a three-story brick building. Offering thirty beds, Walden became Chattanooga's first hospital to be owned, run and staffed by African Americans, and dedicated to their treatment. There, Wheeler would practice medicine and train nurses for more than twenty years. When Walden Hospital finally closed in 1952, it was converted into apartments. Dr. Wheeler died in 1957, but her building still stands, and a state historic marker identifies the site of Walden Hospital, and her lifelong dedication and devotion to her profession and her people.

Chattanooga is the birthplace of many notable African Americans in the arts. In 1894, the legendary Bessie Smith was born here, destined to become acknowledged as one of the greatest of the blues singers. Although the "Empress of the Blues" tragically perished in an automobile accident in 1937, she was posthumously elected to the Rock n' Roll Hall of Fame.

Sam Gooden and Fred Cash, Howard High School alumni, formed a singing group called the *Impressions*. For their fifteen successive smash hits, they joined Bessie Smith in the Rock n' Roll Hall of Fame in 1991.

In 1897, young Roland Hayes, ten years old, moved to Chattanooga. Hayes, the son of former slaves, was discovered singing on the streets in town by a music teacher, who offered him free lessons. This world-class tenor would become the first African American to sing at Carnegie Hall, perform for England's royal family and achieve stardom of international proportions. He toured Europe several times, sang in seven languages and was the highest-paid tenor in the world. Hayes's concerts always included spirituals, for which he arranged their orchestral accompaniment.

Samuel L. Jackson, world-renown contemporary actor, is a graduate of Chattanooga's Riverside High School. One of Hollywood's most successful stars, he has been nominated for the Oscar, and has been recognized by the Cannes Film Festival. Jackson continues to star in top box office films.

These names represent but a few of the extraordinary lives to be discovered at Chattanooga's impressive African American Museum, at 200 East Martin Luther King Boulevard. Established in 1983, its varied collections are housed in a handsome contemporary brick building that occupies the site of the

World-famous Empress of the Blues, Bessie Smith, was born in Chattanooga in 1894.
Courtesy of the Library of Congress, Prints & Photographs Division, Carl Van Vechten Collection.

former fifty-room Martin Hotel, built in 1924. The Martin was the largest African American hotel in the South, once hosting such notables as Ella Fitzgerald, Lena Horne, Mahalia Jackson and Nat King Cole. This historic hotel was demolished in 1986.

A striking glass atrium divides the new building, with the museum on one side and the Bessie Smith Performance Hall on the other. The 264-seat performance hall is host to outstanding jazz and blues concerts, and is also available to be booked for meetings and events. (Danny Toney may be contacted at 423.704.7812 for information regarding upcoming performances.)

Museum tour guide Joyce Terrell (grandniece of Bessie Smith) became the first African American student to integrate the public schools in Prince William County, Virginia, in 1961 at age thirteen. She describes the terror of her home being shot at, and the isolation she experienced during that time of unrest, in her soon-to-be published book, *A Blues Song of My Own*. Terrell's father, Reverend James P. Russell, now eighty-six, was president of the NAACP, and married to Lillian Smith Russell, daughter of Bessie Smith's brother.

This vibrant museum offers insight into early African history, as well as a view of the past two centuries of local African American experience. Chattanooga's part in the civil rights movement of the 1960s is well defined. The museum also offers remarkable insight into Chattanooga's unexpected influence on the life of Dr. Martin Luther King prior to the civil rights movement.

According to one staff member, Dr. King had applied for a pastor's position at First Baptist Church on Eighth Street, a relatively conservative church. Because he was considered too progressive, he was turned down. As this staff member stated, "Imagine what might never have taken place—the impact on history—if his application had been accepted!"

Even so, Dr. King liked spending time in Chattanooga, and frequently visited the area. The conclusion of his now-famous "I have a dream" speech refers to the city's looming landmark feature: "Let freedom ring from Lookout Mountain of Tennessee...From every mountainside, let freedom ring..."

Impeccably organized and visitor-friendly, this award-winning museum is one of Chattanooga's gems. (Call 423.266.8658 for hours.)

THE FIREMEN'S
MEMORIAL FOUNTAIN

In town.

One of downtown Chattanooga's most handsome and familiar landmarks is the Firemen's Memorial Fountain at 631 Georgia Avenue. The figure was set in place in 1888 to honor those firemen who had lost their lives in service to their community.

In the latter part of the nineteenth century, monuments to firemen became a popular subject for public memorials, some being carved of marble, others cast in bronze and later the less costly zinc. The J.L. Mott Iron Works of New York supplied many of these statues, and is believed to be the source for the Chattanooga memorial. Mott offered cast-iron fountain bases, on which the zinc statues were to be placed.

The Chattanooga statue is cast in the style of the fireman holding a hose, and while the original one of zinc had to be replaced with an aluminum replica in 1961 due to deterioration, old photographs show very little difference between the old and newer version. The faithful restoration ensures that Chattanooga's brave fireman will continue to honor the courage of firefighters for generations yet to come.

THE JEWISH COMMUNITY IN EARLY CHATTANOOGA

In town.

Chattanooga has been the home of a vital Jewish community since the Civil War. The earliest Jewish families to arrive here came during the second wave of Jewish emigration from Europe, from 1865 to 1880, and the third wave, from 1881 to 1928.

Chattanooga's oldest and largest congregation, Mizpah Congregation (Reform), was established in 1866 by a group of Western European and German Jewish businessmen, a number of whom were Civil War veterans. Meetings were first held in the home of Jacob and Fannie Bach, who had come from Germany. In 1870, the synagogue established the Mizpah Religious School.

Of Chattanooga's three Jewish congregations, the second oldest is B'Nai Zion, having been founded in 1888. Its origins began in services held in the home of Jewish merchants Wolfe and Dora Brody. Its first synagogue was built in 1902 at the corner of Fourteenth and Carter Streets. In 1931, the congregation moved to a synagogue on Vine Street. While originally an Orthodox congregation, in 1959 it became Conservative.

In 1974, the B'Nai Zion congregation built a modern synagogue at 114 McBrien Road, which they occupy today. This chapel contains the historic Arks, Golden Lions and Eternal Light from their two earlier synagogues.

Chattanooga's Orthodox Beth Sholom Synagogue was established in 1959 by former members of B'Nai Zion. In 1977, after its headquarters were bombed by a hate crime terrorist, who was caught and served time in prison, a new synagogue was constructed in the Brainerd area.

The Chattanooga area has had three other early Jewish congregations, which are now disbanded: the Orthodox Shaari-Zion and the Yiddish Culture

Chattanooga Workman's Circle Congregation, whose members operated a school. Because of their background in Soviet Russia, where religion was illegal, the Workman's Circle emphasized the teaching of Yiddish rather than Hebrew. Both of these congregations broke up due to the west side renewal and freeway projects.

The third and less traditional expression of local Jewish history was the Alabama Sand Mountain Kibbutz, which was founded in 1903 by Jacob Daneman. An idealist, Daneman envisioned a farming community supported by a group-owned shirt factory, whose members would work together and share in the wealth. But due to the commune's remote location, poor soil and the failure of the shirt factory, the community did not prosper and disbanded after only two years. However, its short life gave it the distinction of being the first kibbutz in America.

Mizpah Congregation, the oldest of Chattanooga's existing Jewish congregations, has met in three sanctuaries, the first of which was the Temple at 429 Walnut Street, built in 1882. In 1904, a second Temple, designed by J.S. Moudy, was dedicated at the corner of Oak and Lindsay Streets. This classic-influenced building still stands, although the congregation moved again in 1928 when Adolph Ochs donated a larger and magnificent third Temple at 923 McCallie Avenue, built in honor of his parents. This building is now on the Tennessee Historic Registry, and contains significant examples of religious art.

The Ten Commandments are carved in marble above the entrance to the sanctuary, and are surrounded by the Lion of Judah, prophets Amos and Hosea and the American eagle. The sanctuary, ornamented with eight stained-glass windows, holds the Ark containing several Torahs, including the Holocaust Torah, donated in 1985. This Torah came from the small Jewish community of Kromerz, whose history began in the twelfth century but ended abruptly in the ethnic cleansing of the Nazi regime.

It is said that Hitler intended to build a Museum of the Extinct Jewish People, displaying all the Torahs and Judaica he had stolen and stored in Prague, while his diabolic schemes for world dominion by an Arian super race were being played out. History, mercifully, was not on his side, and the collection of artifacts was stored for many years. It was eventually sent to London's Westminster Synagogue, whose congregation undertook the refurbishing and redistribution of the precious scrolls.

Other areas of the Mizpah complex contain an exceptional marble statue of Moses, and display cases with historic artifacts. The Jewish Archives of Chattanooga, which includes collections from all of the city's Jewish community, was established in 1999 by Joy Adams, and is located in rooms behind the Mizpah Bima.

The Jewish Community in Early Chattanooga

By the late 1900s, Chattanooga had become a hub of business and industry, and many early shops and businesses were established by members of the Jewish community. Henry Schwarz, a Hungarian immigrant, came to Chattanooga in 1875, opening Schwartz Brothers Shoe Store at 812 Market Street. In 1904, Charles Rosenthal would open his clothing store in the same building.

Herman Cohn established his Violet Studio Shop in 1915, which continued well into the 1990s (its name changed to Violet Camera Shop), located on Seventh Street. In 1919, Phil Angel and Henry Morris founded the Angel Printing Company, which operated for seventy-two years. In 1920, Abe and Lou Effron opened Effron's Department Store at Sixth and Market Streets. It was known as "the Home of Low Prices." There have been many more successful contributions to the city's growth by Chattanooga's Jewish entrepreneurs—bakeries, groceries, cleaners, restaurants, jewelry and candy stores, to list but a few.

But Chattanooga's Jewish community has also had more than its share of civic-minded citizens. In 1917, two brothers, Mose and Garrison Siskin, joined their father Robert in the steel business. Sons of Lithuanian immigrants, the Siskins early on became interested in assisting the physically handicapped. By the 1950s, they had given thousands of dollars to create the Siskin Foundation, which offers hope and rehabilitation to the disabled. The foundation's newest hospital opened in 1990 near Erlanger Hospital. In 1996, the Siskins received the Ellis Island Medal of Honor, given to immigrant families who have made a difference in America.

In addition to their contribution to health, the Siskins established the Siskin Museum of Religious Artifacts in 1950. It is located at 1101 Carter Street in town, in the front lobby of the Siskin Children's Institute.

The museum houses over four hundred significant artifacts from many cultures, including those acquired in the 1950s by Rabbi Swift, who was sent by the Siskins to retrieve early Judaica and other religious relics that had been brought to Great Britain by Jewish refugees and others fleeing the Nazi regime.

The museum contains Torah scrolls, Haggadah manuscripts, silver spice boxes, Madonnas, a Fabergé egg and Eastern religious items, including a fourteenth-century Buddha. (For more information on the Siskin Museum of Religious Artifacts, call 423.634.1700.)

One of Mizpah Congregation's early members was Dr. Marx Block. Born in France in 1832, he immigrated to the United States and studied medicine in Chicago. He served in the Union army as an assistant surgeon with the Fourteenth Colored Regiment. After the war, he practiced medicine in Chattanooga until 1869, when his health began to decline.

Forming a partnership with his brother-in-law, Prosper Lazard, Dr. Block opened a retail drug business, which would soon become a wholesale trade as well. Lazard had come from Lorraine, France, and was the earliest of Chattanooga's Jews to serve in public office. Although he was appointed police commissioner in 1887, and later was elected city treasurer, Lazard also entertained an entrepreneurial spirit. When his in-town floating bathhouse on the Tennessee River was swept downstream in the 1867 flood and had to be towed back, Lazard must have considered the opening of a drug business to be a much safer and sounder venture.

Together, Block and Lazard created their own brands, and also offered a wine made from grapes grown by Block on his small farm on Missionary Ridge.

In 1883, Block purchased property at the corner of Market and Seventh Streets, and constructed a handsome office building, designed by architect Adrian DeLisle. A century later, the building was acquired by Cornerstones Incorporated, a preservation organization that restored and donated it to the United Way. The Block Building stands as one of the city's finer examples of Victorian commercial architecture.

Another of Chattanooga's early businessmen was David Bernard Loveman (Leibman), born in the Austrian Empire in 1844. Immigrating to the United States in 1853, Loveman lived and worked in several cities before coming to Chattanooga in 1875. Here, he purchased a small dry goods store, which grew in size over the years to become Loveman's Department Store.

In 1884, the company purchased land on the southeast corner of Eighth and Market Streets, where Loveman constructed a handsome four-story building. Five years later, the store was destroyed by fire, but the business would continue on to become Chattanooga's premier department store for the next hundred years.

Following the fire, a new five-story brick Loveman's Building, designed by Samuel Patton, was constructed in 1893. Although the store is no longer in operation, the building remains, and is now restored and divided into condominiums.

The retail business remained in the Loveman family until 1932, when it was purchased by Colonel Richard L. Moore, father of the renowned opera singer, Grace Moore.

ADOLPH OCHS

A Man of the Times

An extraordinary journalist, Adolph S. Ochs was a member of Chattanooga's historic Mizpah Congregation. This philanthropist and publisher of the *Chattanooga Times* would ultimately rescue the failing *New York Times* and make it into the standard of American newspapers.

Born in Cincinnati in 1858, Ochs was the son of educated German immigrants. From observing the differences of his parents, whose views on the Civil War were diametrically opposed, Ochs grew into a young man who valued tolerance. After his family moved to Knoxville following the Civil War, Ochs began his future career in journalism and publishing by delivering newspapers.

From this inauspicious beginning, he moved to a position as printer's devil, eventually becoming a master of composition. He worked for a time on the *Louisville Courier-Journal*, and in July 1879, at the age of twenty, he purchased on a shoestring a controlling share of the *Chattanooga Times*. Under his stewardship, it would become one of the most outstanding papers in the South, and in 1892, Ochs constructed the handsome six-story Chattanooga Times Building at the corner of Georgia Avenue and East Eighth Street. With its gilt, domed observation tower and circular window, which marked Ochs's office, the building served as home to the *Chattanooga Times* until 1942. Known today as the Dome Building, it has been remodeled for offices, and remains an important city landmark.

As a reporter, Ochs subjugated his personal opinions and political leanings, stressing instead a nonpartisan approach to journalism; the appeal of his paper rested on its well-written fairness. A tireless worker, Ochs became a great supporter of his paper's hometown, founding its public library, helping to create the Chickamauga Battlefield Military Park and contributing much to Chattanooga's Reform congregation.

He was also to play a strong role in the development of Lookout Mountain, the Ochs Highway and the Ochs Observatory in Lookout Mountain's Point Park bearing his name. The *Chattanooga Times* published its last issue on January 4, 1999, when Ochs's heirs sold the paper to its long-standing rival, the *Chattanooga Free Press*.

In 1896, Ochs took over the struggling *New York Times*, which was destined to become one of the world's leading newspapers. Cutting the paper's price from three cents to one per issue, he competed financially with the tabloid papers he detested without lowering his paper's standards. In 1904, New York City's Times Square was named for his paper, whose offices had recently moved to its new location on Forty-second Street. A fireworks gala on New Year's Eve celebrated the event.

Giving the *New York Times* its famous slogan, "All the news that's fit to print," Ochs would ultimately take his place beside the great journalists of his day. Adolph Ochs died in Chattanooga on April 8, 1935, on a visit to the beloved city he had so generously helped build.

THE LOSS OF CITICO MOUND

In town.

The progress of civilization often extracts a price from the past, with thoughtless and irreparable results. Today, careful study and exacting care would have been used during the construction of Chattanooga's Amnicola Highway, also known as Riverside Drive or Highway 58, which follows the banks of the Tennessee River, leading east from downtown.

But when construction of the road was begun in June, 1915, steam shovels and wagons laden with earth began their task of removing large portions of the ancient Hamilton County landmark known as Citico Mound. Shaped like a great serpent, the mound was the remainder of a Mississippian town established near Citico Creek, and dated AD 1000–1500. Built by a race of prehistoric people, Citico Mound, measuring a hundred feet in length and forty feet high, was also a burial site. But in 1915, it was not afforded the respect as such.

The mound was located in proximity to the present Tennessee American Water Company's Distribution Complex. The irony is that, had a slight shift in the survey of Riverside Drive been made prior to construction, the tragic loss of this wealth of early Tennessee prehistory could have been spared.

The mound's first known exploration was done in 1865, when M.O. Read tunneled into it. Read's account, which appears in the Smithsonian Report of 1867, states that he encountered skeletal remains in its base, and postholes that indicated that some sort of structure had once been present.

The mound was next explored by archaeologist Charles B. Moore for the Philadelphia Academy of Science. He headed a party that was engaged in exploring prehistoric sites along the Tennessee River. His men sunk a shaft twelve feet down into the mound, but when Moore failed to discover remains, his report incorrectly concluded that "the mound was domicilliary and not a burial mound."

But in 1915, highway workmen discovered that Moore had missed, by a few feet, a burial containing a copper crown and a quantity of large shell beads, likely to have once belonged to a king or chief of these ancient people. The items were soon afterward acquired by collector and archaeologist W.E. Myer of Carthage, Tennessee.

In 1932, Chattanooga collector Charles Peacock described portions of a pot in his own collection, which had been removed from the mound after the steam shovel's intrusion. His description, in his own words, reads: "Part of a square scallop-rimmed pot, of light tan clay, highly decorated with red pigment." Peacock believed the design to be Aztec, hinting at a relationship between the builders of Citico Mound and the early natives of Mexico. He stated that a round vessel of similar design had been found by Moore "on the Bennett place near the lock and dam on the Tennessee River."

Peacock believed the copper crown to be "made of copper found in its native, malleable state. The mineral was traded to Indians in this locality by those of the Lake Superior region. The copper found here is impure, and [malleable copper] could only be obtained by smelting, a process unknown to these people." Other copper artifacts were recovered from Citico Mound, including arrowheads, tomahawks and a copper bowl.

Among other articles Peacock discovered at Citico Mound were perforated bear claws, a polished wolf's jawbone, a conch shell water dipper, flint implements, stone celts, deer antlers, gaming stones and shell beads.

One particularly remarkable artifact unearthed at Citico was a small clay effigy, which appeared to be an armored head of a horse, and had most likely adorned the rim of a pot. The head stirred considerable interest among local historians in the 1930s, as it was thought that the horse had not been known to American Indians before white contact, De Soto's expedition having come through the area sometime around 1539. Was it possible that one of Citico's pottery makers, who were usually women, might have seen De Soto's armored horses, and been inspired to replicate one in clay?

Shell gorgets, or breastplates, engraved with a rattlesnake design, were also found in Citico Mound. The conch shells from which these ornaments were made had been acquired through trade with coastal peoples.

In the 1700s, the ancient town at Citico Mound was part of Cherokee lands. During the outset of the Civil War, the mound became a fort and lookout position. But following the battles for Chattanooga, Union soldiers used Citico Mound as a rest and recreation spot. They constructed benches and an observation tower at its top, and a wooden gangplank for boating and fishing along the adjacent riverbank.

At war's end, vibrations from the guns fired to celebrate Lee's surrender caused the collapse of a tunnel that had been dug into the mound by soldiers searching for relics. The sunken earth revealed skeletal remains. In 1929, the East Tennessee Archaeological Society excavated below the base of the mound, and encountered more burials.

It is believed that as many as ten thousand burials were uncovered at Citico, one as recently as 1989. A great number of these, along with dirt from the mound, were summarily shoved into the Tennessee River during the building of Amnicola Highway and the subsequent construction of an emerging city.

Only the river remains to remember the ancient ones who built a mountain with their own hands, from which to view its majesty, and commemorate their dead. Perhaps it is good that we remember them, too, and ask a silent pardon as we pass along our modern highway where their great civilization once flourished.

GRACE MOORE

Tennessee's Incomparable Songbird

Forest Hills Cemetery, St. Elmo, Tennessee, four miles southwest of town.

From the obscurity of a small east Tennessee town, she rose to international fame, flared like a rocket across the Hollywood skies, and dazzled millions from Carnegie Hall to Paris with her extraordinary voice. Today, she rests beside her father in Chattanooga's peaceful Forest Hills Cemetery, at the foot of Lookout Mountain.

The eldest child of Richard Lawson Moore and Tessie Jane Stokely Moore of North Carolina, Mary Willie Grace Moore was born on December 5, 1898, in tiny Del Rio, Tennessee, near the North Carolina border.

With thick auburn hair and brilliant blue eyes, Grace's irrepressible personality made itself apparent early. Her grandfather taught her to sing and dance at local square dances, but her father, a hard-shell Baptist, strongly disapproved. Although personality differences marked Grace's stormy relationship with her father throughout life, the loving bonds between them remained indestructible, even in death.

Grace loved the family farm, and reveled in country life. She was known for her singing ability by the time she was seven, and her mother was encouraged to find training for her. But Grace's mother was occupied with birthing and burying children. Four of Grace's siblings would die before reaching adulthood, leaving only Grace, her sister Emily and two brothers, Richard Jr. and James.

Grace's father moved the family to Jellico, Tennessee. As the senior Moore prospered, he was criticized by locals who resented his doing business with minorities. For this, and for his family's reputation of being somewhat contentious, the Moores were not accepted by many of Jellico's conservative residents. This did not keep Grace's father from becoming active in politics. He

Grace Moore received an Oscar nomination for her semiautobiographical role in the 1930s musical *One Night of Love*.

made influential friendships, and for his political participation, the honorary title of colonel was bestowed on him by Tennessee's Governor Rye.

The Moores attended Jellico's First Baptist Church, where Grace sang in the choir. Her tomboy side remained equally strong well into high school, where she became captain of the basketball team. One colorful incident, revealing Grace's hot temper, was marked by a physical catfight with another player in which she lost her pants on the court and swore audibly when the game was called.

Grace spent much time at the local movie house, indulging her dreams of becoming a film star like Mary Pickford. As she grew into the beautiful, adventurous woman that would win hearts worldwide, many young men in Jellico sought her company.

Let it be said that Grace did much to provoke her stern and exacting father. Their relationship remained tempestuous, and Colonel Moore was usually frustrated in efforts to control his eldest daughter. But Grace was a free spirit, no doubt sensing the great destiny that awaited her.

In 1916, after being made to publicly repent before the church for dancing, Grace convinced her father to send her to Ward-Belmont College in Nashville. There she began her first formal training in music, but her rustic background made it difficult for her to adjust. She was expelled for inappropriate behavior in 1917.

Undaunted, she next enrolled in the Wilson-Greene School of Music, where she first met her idol, Mary Garden, lead soprano of the Chicago

Grace Moore

Opera. Overwhelmed, Grace knelt and kissed Garden's hand, informing her that she, too, would one day be a great singer.

At twenty-one, Grace moved to New York City, began singing in smoky cafes and lost her voice entirely. Desperate, she sought out Enrico Caruso's doctor, who informed her that nightclub singing had ruined her voice, and she must not even speak for three months. Grace secluded herself in a Canadian cabin, vowing to devote herself to serious music.

Then she accepted a lead in a New York musical, in which she sang "First You Wiggle, Then You Waggle," Grace punctuating the lyrics with appropriate motions. Although her stern father was in the audience, she managed to keep him supportive of her blossoming career.

Grace became part of New York's theatrical and literary circles, and made important friendships with Jerome Kern and George Gershwin. When advised to change her name to something more European and exotic, she flatly refused, stating that she meant to become famous as Grace Moore, American.

She sailed to France in 1924, where she hobnobbed in Paris with the likes of Noel Coward and Cole Porter. She met twice with Mary Garden, who promised to arrange an audition for the Opera Comique if Grace would master the title role of *Louise*. But when Irving Berlin invited her to star in his Music Box Revue, she accepted, and sailed for New York.

The reviews were flattering to Grace, but her sights were set on the Metropolitan Opera. She obtained two successive auditions, but failed both. Grace wrote to Mary Garden, asking how she might prepare for a third audition. Garden graciously offered Grace her luxurious Monte Carlo apartment and lessons with her personal voice coach.

Grace passed her third audition, and debuted at the Met on February 7, 1928, in the role of Mimi in *La Boheme*. A retinue of Tennessee family and friends witnessed her twenty-five curtain calls. Grace Moore had at last arrived, but she was only beginning.

Another dream would be partly fulfilled in 1931, when she starred in MGM's *A Lady's Morals*, a biography of Jenny Lind, the "Swedish Nightingale." It flopped, and when her second film, *New Moon*, did little better, Grace was dropped by the studio. To recoup, she sailed for Europe; onboard she met a handsome Spaniard, Valentín Parrera. They married in Cannes on July 15, 1931.

But fortune smiled again, and Grace, the original comeback kid, was signed by Columbia to star in a musical, *One Night of Love*. The script contained many details from Grace's life, was an overwhelming success and captured for Grace an Academy Award nomination for Best Actress.

The movie catapulted Grace to national fame, and she was constantly in demand for concerts and radio appearances. Over four thousand people attended her November 1934 concert in Chattanooga. Grace was thrilled to perform for her father, who had moved to town a few years earlier to oversee his newly acquired Loveman's Department Store. Chattanooga's mayor proclaimed a "Grace Moore Week," but an even more outstanding honor was hers when she became the first woman to be awarded the title of Tennessee Colonel—a rank she now shared with her beloved father.

In 1935, she began a weekly radio show, and was awarded the gold medal by the Society of Arts and Science. More dear to her was Mary Garden's public statement that Grace Moore was the only singer whose talent was equal to her own. Grace performed *La Boheme* at the Met seventeen times, starred in *Louise* at the Paris Opera Comique and made four more American films.

In 1940, Grace and Val Parrera purchased a 1797 home in New England, where she wrote her autobiography, *You're Only Human Once*. To help overcome the preferential treatment given to European artists, Grace founded the Grace Moore School of Singing to mentor American singers. One of her first students was Dorothy Kirsten, future Metropolitan Opera star, whom Grace considered to be her successor. Grace's legacy to aspiring singers continues through the University of Tennessee's voice scholarship offered in her name.

A true citizen of the world, Grace considered herself an American first, volunteering to entertain Allied troops at home and abroad during World War Two, often paying her own expenses before the USO was formally established.

In 1944, Grace attended her father's funeral in Chattanooga, expressing a wish to be buried beside him in beautiful Forest Hills Cemetery in St. Elmo, at the foot of Lookout Mountain. She had no way of knowing that, unlike her previous wishes, this one was to be fulfilled much sooner than she would have preferred.

On January 25, 1947, Grace sang a successful concert in Copenhagen, Denmark. The following day, she boarded a Dutch KLM plane that crashed on the runway, killing all onboard. Val Parerra and Grace's brother Jim brought her body back by rail to Chattanooga, where thousands of mourners crowded the grounds of First Baptist Church for a final farewell. Grace Moore now rests beside her father in her native Tennessee.

In 1963, Hollywood paid tribute to Grace in the biographical film, *So This is Love*, starring Kathryn Grayson. More recently, a musical titled, *The Tennessee Nightingale*, adapted from Grace's autobiography, debuted at the Barter Theatre in Abingdon, Virginia.

The Tennessee Songbird's voice is silent, save for rare, treasured recordings. But her contributions to art and music remain as lasting testimony to the passionate, tenacious dreams of a fiery young east Tennessee girl from the humble hills of Del Rio.

DRAGGING CANOE

Fiercest Warrior of the Cherokee

Of all the later Cherokees to war against the white invasion of Indian lands, none was more formidable than this son of the famous Cherokee diplomat Attakullakulla, who was known among the whites as Little Carpenter. Tall, smallpox-scarred Tsi'yu-gunsini, or Dragging Canoe, was born in 1734 in Monroe County, Tennessee.

It is said that this name was given to him as a youth when he attempted to join a war party by towing a canoe, which he could only drag along. The name signified his fierce determination to fight, and was an early indication of the man he would become, whose life was to impact both races. Although the seat of his greatest power would eventually be established on the Tennessee River, a few miles south of today's Chattanooga, his early adult life took place in northeast Tennessee.

On March 17, 1775, in protest to the theft of Cherokee lands lost through the Treaty of Sycamore Shoals, Dragging Canoe declared to Colonel Henderson that his ill-gotten prize would be a dark and bloody ground. He then declared war on all whites that intruded into sovereign Indian territories. At the treaty's conclusion, Dragging Canoe rose to condemn the selling of Cherokee lands:

> *Whole Indian nations have melted away before the white man's advance. They leave scarcely a name of our people except those wrongly recorded. Where are the Delawares? They have been reduced to a mere shadow of their former greatness....Now the white men have passed the mountains, and settled upon Cherokee land. They wish to have that action sanctioned by treaty...When that is gained, the same spirit will lead them upon other land of the Cherokees. New cessions will be asked. Finally the whole country, which the Cherokees and their fathers have so long occupied, will*

be demanded, and the remnant of Ani-Yunwiya, THE REAL PEOPLE, once so great and formidable, will be compelled to seek refuge in some distant wilderness.

There they will stay only a short while, until they again behold the advancing banners of the same greedy host…[when] the extinction of the whole race will be proclaimed. Should we not therefore run all risks, and incur all consequences, rather than submit to further loss of our country? Such treaties may be alright for men who are too old to hunt or fight. As for me, I have my young warriors about me. We will have our lands. A-WANINSKI, I have spoken.

These were no empty words, for Dragging Canoe would spend the rest of his life fulfilling this declaration. During the American Revolution, the Cherokee resisted American infiltration by siding with the British, and Dragging Canoe conducted a main attack. Again in 1776, The Canoe led seven hundred Cherokees in two separate attacks against United States forts—Eaton's Station and Fort Watauga in North Carolina.

When his father and Oconostata ceased their warfare, following the utter devastation of the Cherokee Middle and Lower towns by John Sevier's troops, Dragging Canoe formed his own band from the upper Overhill Cherokee settlements, and relocated these people south, where he built eleven towns along South Chickamauga Creek, near present-day Chattanooga. Operating from these sites, these disaffected Cherokees continued their warfare against the whites. Dragging Canoe's group of ferocious warriors became known as the Chickamaugans.

In 1779, Dragging Canoe spoke to the Shawnee, seeking to ensure that tribe's unity with the Cherokee in fighting against the advancing destruction of the southern tribes. Even today, his bold words of encouragement resound through the centuries as a cry of triumph for all native peoples: "We are not yet conquered!"

In 1782, the Chickamauga towns were destroyed, sending Dragging Canoe and his band farther south, where they settled into the Five Lower Towns near the Tennessee River Gorge. These were Running Water, Nickajack, Long Island on the Tennessee River, Crow Town and Lookout Mountain Town, near present-day Trenton, Georgia. Due to Dragging Canoe's success in enlisting bands of Creek and Shawnee to join him, he commanded over a thousand warriors, and would become the most significant threat to white colonists in the contested South.

The Tennessee River slices deeply through the Cumberland Mountains at Chattanooga, its turbulent, descending waters carving out steep cliffs on both sides. Stretches of rapids, and a treacherous whirlpool known as the Suck, made navigation by boat a deadly prospect. (With the construction of the Chickamauga Dam, this whirlpool is today submerged.) From this extensive natural fortress, Dragging Canoe continued to fight his guerrilla war against the white colonists.

Although the British surrendered in 1783, Dragging Canoe and his Chickamaugan Confederacy continued their attacks against white encroachment until his death in 1792.

White settlements along the Holston, Nolichucky and Watauga Rivers, and later the Cumberland River, were all attacked by Dragging Canoe's consolidated band of warriors. Five of Dragging Canoe's brothers—The Raven, The Badger, Tachee, Little Owl and Turtle at Home—sometimes took part in these raids.

Interestingly enough, Dragging Canoe's cousin, the peace-loving Beloved Woman, Nancy Ward, on two occasions warned the whites of his coming raids. If ever two members of the same family were polar opposites, it was surely this pair, as exemplified by the diversity in their choice of service to their people.

Up to the last year of his life, Dragging Canoe would remain on good terms with the British. Their appreciation of his friendship during the Revolution was strongly evidenced when one of his brothers returned from Detroit with numerous English gifts for the intrepid warrior.

The Canoe sympathized considerably with the Shawnee in their efforts to stave off white encroachment, and was asked by the Creek Chief McGillivray to help form a larger confederacy of southern tribes for the purpose of mutual survival. It was hoped that Dragging Canoe might even recruit the support of the Chickasaw Chief Piomingo, who had made an alliance with the United States. Dragging Canoe met with the chiefs of the neighboring tribes, and all pledged cooperation. The exception was Piomingo, who ultimately rejected the offer.

Upon returning from this alliance-seeking mission—a pattern later pursued by the great Tecumseh in seeking to unite the western tribes— Dragging Canoe attended strenuous all-night dances at Lookout Mountain Town, celebrating his brother's recent victory over a Cumberland River settlement. Most reports indicate that he suffered a heart attack there, or died of exhaustion, but others suggest an untended wound as the cause of death.

After seventeen years of war against the white intruders, his mortal enemy, Dragging Canoe was no more.

Some tribal elders of his time considered Dragging Canoe a renegade for not submitting to their authority. The white settlers called him a barbaric murderer, and history has, in the main, proclaimed him a savage brute. But truth is not always so easy to define or dismiss. That the Canoe's life was written in violent bloodshed cannot be denied. That he and his band engaged in the slaughter of innocent women and children is also fact. Yet who among us would not believe our homeland and our way of life worthy of defending, and would simply surrender it to foreign invaders without a fight?

It has been said that Dragging Canoe's powerful resistance won white respect and held off their surging encroachment long enough for Cherokee culture to flourish, as it profoundly did in the early nineteenth century. Today's Cherokee descendants in Oklahoma and North Carolina proudly preserve that culture, and to many, Dragging Canoe is a patriotic hero, engaging in relentless battles against the forces that were seeking to annihilate his people and culture.

More than a few historians consider him the most influential Native American to come from the Southeastern United States. His defiant resistance would provide a model for nineteenth-century Native American leaders in their courageous efforts to stop the white supplanting of their people.

At the Cherokee council of Estanaula, held in June 1792, Black Fox spoke these unlikely words in honor of Dragging Canoe: "The Dragging Canoe has left the world. He was a man of consequence in his country. He was a friend both to his own and the white people."

A CASTLE IN THE CLOUDS

Lookout Mountain, seven miles southwest of town.

For eighty years it has graced Lookout Mountain's distant horizon above Chattanooga. Its intriguing silhouette viewed from the deep valleys below suggests the mystery of medieval times, or a fabulous fairyland kingdom. Shrouded in mists, the magnificent structure began its odyssey as the Lookout Mountain Hotel. Located on a high point known as Jackson Hill on the mountain's west side, the edifice was constructed in 1928 by Garnet Carter, a local entrepreneur of many talents.

A succession of hostelries on Lookout preceded the construction of this hotel, but most of these were long gone by 1928. An earlier Lookout Mountain Hotel, located near 311 East Brow Road, was constructed in 1858 when the area was then known as Summertown. Thought to have been the first hostelry on the mountain, it was occupied by both Federal and Confederate troops, and although it survived the Civil War, it burned to the ground in 1908.

A still earlier structure, located on the east brow of the summit, had been built by George D. Foster, who was nicknamed "the Old Man of the Mountain" by visiting Union Generals Hooker and Sherman. Foster's home was turned into a hotel in 1887. Although Foster was a Union man, the lumber for this building had been carried up the mountain on the backs of slaves. Later known as Lookout Mountain House, it burned down on July 1, 1921.

A third hostelry, the four-story Point Hotel, was constructed in 1885 at the terminal of the first Incline Railway on the mountain. For two and a half dollars to four dollars per night, guests could enjoy its billiard room and bathhouse, until the hotel was eventually torn down and the first incline abandoned.

In 1890, the massive, imposing Lookout Inn was built, sprawling 365 feet in length, rising above and across from the Incline Station Number Two. It boasted 365 rooms—one foot of frontage, and one room for each day of the year. Railroad cars full of guests were brought up the mountain over broad-gauge tracks, and stopped directly in front of the hotel, which soon became one of the most popular resorts in the South. The inn dominated the east side of the mountain until it, too, was destroyed by fire in November, 1908, and was never rebuilt.

Joseph P. McCullough, an early investor in Lookout Mountain's real estate, had built the McCullough Hotel at the mountain's Natural Bridge. Its name was later changed to the Natural Bridge Hotel in 1884, when the property was purchased by the Spiritualist Church. Discretely situated approximately a mile from Sunset Rock, the hotel came into favor as a Spiritualist retreat, until it was sold in 1890. Due to its less prominent location, and the development of more commercial sites on the mountain, the Natural Bridge, its hotel and nearby spring gradually fell into disuse, eventually becoming neglected by tourists.

By 1928, a void clearly existed in Lookout's ability to welcome and house visitors and make use of their potential business trade, thus setting the stage for the emergence of another fine hotel atop this beautiful mountain, irresistible to so many. Enter Garnet Carter.

A shrewd businessman, Carter successfully acquired the backing of an Atlanta company for his plan, and his grand hotel was constructed for almost $1.5 million—a considerable investment for the times. Sparing no luxury for its guests, the hotel offered swimming, tennis, horseback riding, dancing, hiking and fine cuisine.

Carter and his wife Frieda—who had designed a number of fantastic, eclectic buildings in Lookout Mountain's Fairyland development—would later open the now-famous "Rock City" landmark on the east brow of the mountain in 1932.

The Carter gift for creative thinking was also possessed by Garnet's brother, Paul, who helped him open the first miniature Tom Thumb golf courses on Lookout Mountain in 1928. Within two years, more than a thousand of these miniature golf courses had been successfully franchised, both nationally and internationally, giving rise to the family sport that still enjoys popularity to this day.

Located on Scenic Highway, some five miles south of Point Park, Garnet Carter constructed a majestic and conspicuous landmark—its extended roofline and rising 412-foot tower, with a flashing beacon located at top, was visible for miles around. Seven states can be observed from its top. Carter's

A Castle in the Clouds

Lookout Mountain Hotel contained two hundred guest rooms, and its unique positioning offered spectacular views of the valleys below from both sides of the mountain. But despite its auspicious beginnings, such a grand venture would prove ill-timed.

The Lookout Mountain Hotel held its grand opening in 1928, only one year before the disastrous stock market crash of 1929, which devastated the fortunes of many who chose to frequent these grand hotels. Nevertheless, Carter's hotel held on for a few years, wavering before finally closing its doors in the early 1930s, when the Great Depression dealt the hotel industry its final deathblow.

In the next few decades, the hotel would undergo a series of attempts at reopening under various names and owners, and was also reputedly the site of illegal alcohol and gambling during the Prohibition era. Within this lengthy period of varied efforts at revival, the struggling hotel continued to intermittently host guests and events. In November 1938, a five-dollar-per-

The former Castle in the Clouds Hotel, now part of Covenant College, appears through the mists of Lookout Mountain.

Framed 1928 poster, announcing the hotel's grand opening, hangs in a hallway of Carter Hall.

plate luncheon, inviting locals to meet with President Franklin Roosevelt on the premises, was held in its massive dining room.

Still, the grand hotel frequently languished in disuse, and its final reincarnation as a hostelry took place in 1957, when it was given the name of Castle in the Clouds, where local legend reports that film actress Elizabeth Taylor and her fourth husband Eddie Fisher once spent the night.

But even Hollywood glitz would not be enough to sustain a viable business. In 1964, the property was acquired by Covenant College, of Presbyterian Church in America, and this good news was well received by many Chattanoogans, who had become concerned for the welfare and future of the beloved local landmark.

Renovations were made to the structure, and it was rechristened Carter Hall, slated to become the vital center of Covenant's campus activities. The magnificent dark beam and plaster Tudor-style interior has been lovingly restored, its massive timbers and fireplace welcoming. The school's bookstore, housed in one of the downstairs rooms, offers books for sale on local history and the Carter family. In the ensuing years since the property's acquisition, Carter Hall has been joined by a library, a chapel, academic buildings, dormitories and athletic buildings, all providing a rich and attractive campus for its growing student body.

A Castle in the Clouds

Interior of the old hotel, today known as Carter Hall for its original owner and builder. Massive beams and arts and crafts–style furnishings recall the hotel's glory days.

Carter Hall, the former Lookout Mountain Hotel, no longer provides lodging for guests unaffiliated with Covenant College. However, the school has purchased a group of comfortable cottages nestled on a nearby bluff along Scenic Highway, which provide a spectacular view of Chattanooga below, and these are available for rental to the public.

Whether it is the light of early dawn penetrating the ever-present mists of this ancient mountain, or the twinkling of a thousand land-stars glittering through the night from the lighted city far below, the sights will surely be memorable. A visit to Lookout and the mountain's remaining grand lady is well worth the pilgrimage.

ALMOST LOST
—BRAINERD MISSION

Brainerd Road, five miles south of town.

All but crowded out by clamoring civilization, Brainerd Mission's brief but turbulent past sleeps quietly beneath the stones and markers of its tiny cemetery, now jealously guarded by a tall chainlink fence. A large, bustling shopping mall and a paved parking lot have all but erased the scene of one of Chattanooga's earliest historic sites. Only Brainerd's tenacious gravestones remain to tell a small part of the story of this early mission to the Cherokee, and the tragic and courageous events that eventually ended its operations.

In 1816, this property (surrounded and almost devoured today) on the Chickamauga Creek was once a wilderness inhabited by native Cherokees and occasional passing traders. A dense forest covered the land beyond present-day Brainerd, extending over both sides of Missionary Ridge to the outskirts of the city of Chattanooga (not yet known by this name). This present-day city was then but a small Cherokee settlement on the Tennessee River known as Ross's Landing, founded by the parents of statesman and great Cherokee Chief John Ross.

At the council of 1816, to settle boundaries between the Creek and Cherokee Nations, none other than General Andrew Jackson approached the tribal leaders with the intent of introducing schools for their children. When pioneer missionary Cyrus Kingsbury, who literally blazed a trail for later missionaries to follow, addressed the chiefs at that meeting, his proposal for a mission school appeared to be well received by the tribal council.

An elder chief, the Glass, was appointed to assist Kingsbury in selecting a location for the project. Situated on the Chickamauga Creek was acreage belonging to Cherokee Chief John Ross's grandfather, John MacDonald, and it was ultimately chosen as the site to establish a mission and boarding school for the purpose of bringing literacy and the Christian religion to the native peoples.

The challenge of land clearing and construction was undertaken and overseen by Colonel Return J. Meigs, Indian Agent. With the first buildings completed in a matter of months, efforts to "civilize" the Cherokees were officially underway.

In 1817, Kingsbury, Alfred Finney, Mr. and Mrs. Loring Williams and other New England missionaries of the American Board of Foreign Missions, were the first to arrive at the Chickamauga site. This mission staff would change and rotate during its twenty-one years of operation as other missions required their services. Notables among the Brainerd staff were Dr. Samuel A. Worcester, Reverend Ard Hoyt, Dr. Elizur Butler and Charles R. Hicks, whose mother was a full-blood Cherokee. Born in 1767 in the Cherokee town of Tomotley, Hicks served as chief interpreter for over thirty years, and was well respected as one of his tribe's "Beloved Men."

The mission at Chickamauga was rechristened Brainerd Mission in honor of the famous 1700s missionary David Brainerd. But the mission was not particularly well received by the local tribespeople until it became clear that children enrolled there were to receive a well-rounded education. The presiding chiefs at the time were wise enough to understand that their world was rapidly changing—that if they were to survive and compete as a people, their next generation must have a working knowledge of the white man's world. They recognized the power of the white man's written language, and realized it was an all-important tool needed by their children to face an uncertain future.

Despite the paternal attitude of the well-intentioned white missionaries, and some undeniable lack of full understanding and appreciation for native traditions—especially obvious when viewed through our eyes today—there was equally distributed in their hearts a genuine love and admiration for the Creek and Cherokee people. Strong bonds of affection often developed between these missionary teachers and their pupils, and a fierce respect developed among the missionaries for the inherent rights of these tribes, whose future was to come under siege. This respect would be severely tested in years to come.

Many more structures soon rose from the forest floor at Brainerd, including numerous log dwellings for children and visitors, two boys' and girls' schoolhouses, a barn and a two-story mission house connected to a dining hall and kitchen.

A particularly well-finished two-story building for girls' instruction was specifically built at the order of President James Monroe following his visit to the mission in 1819. A log cabin for this purpose was nearly completed when Monroe arrived, but the president had insisted that it was not good enough for the young female students. Therefore, detailed plans for an improved, larger structure were assigned, with a brick or stone chimney and glass windows, to be built at public expense.

A gristmill and sawmill were also constructed, and had begun operating on the Chickamauga. Producing its own crops in gardens and orchards, and raising its own stock, the mission was in the main a self-sustaining community, which, according to an early description by missionary Jeremiah Evarts, occupied little more than fifty acres. In 1819, Brainerd's small, fledgling community was as encompassed by deep woods as it is today surrounded by commerce.

As work at Brainerd progressed, a number of remarkably gifted students gained recognition. Among these was a beautiful young Cherokee woman, Catherine Brown, one of the first Christian converts at the mission. Approximately eighteen, she had arrived at Brainerd on horseback in July 1817, having already learned to speak and read English through her association with a literate Cherokee family.

Because of her refined manners and beauty, and attention to outward appearances, Catherine was at first reluctantly accepted, with doubts that she would not be cut out for the commitment required of Brainerd's students. She was to prove them utterly wrong, becoming a devout star pupil, requesting baptism in 1818, and eventually dedicating herself to teaching others at the newly established Creek Path Mission near her old home.

Her impeccable character and gentle disposition became legendary, and it was revealed that she had once fled her home at night during the Creek War, risking her life to avoid being violated by a contingency of Federal soldiers. But the harsh rigors of constant wilderness travel took their toll, and Catherine succumbed to recurring illness in 1822. Her eloquent personal letters to friends and family were compiled into a book published in 1825, titled, *Memoirs of Catherine Brown, a Christian Indian of the Cherokee Nation.*

Catherine's brother, David Brown (A-wih), assisted in compiling a Cherokee speller, and in 1825, translated a New Testament from the original Greek into Cherokee. Following Hebrew studies at Andover, he returned south to become prominent in the Cherokee Nation and clerk of a delegation in Congress. David Brown died at Creek Path, in 1829.

Elias Boudinot (Kul-le-gee-nah), the nephew of Cherokee leader Major Ridge, enrolled at Brainerd and was from there sent to Cornwall, Connecticut, to continue his studies. He would return in 1827 to become editor of the *Cherokee Phoenix* newspaper in New Echota, Georgia, prior to the Indian Removal. He and his uncle were both murdered in Indian territory for signing the infamous Treaty of New Echota, which ceded the last remaining Indian lands to the whites. The constant persecution of native peoples had caused Boudinot and Ridge to deem this step unavoidable, but its results were disastrous for all.

Many talented students passed through Brainerd's doors, but perhaps the most unlikely of all was a rugged Cherokee man in his early twenties, Atsi, or John Arch. After a life of rough living, Arch's burning desire was to become a scholar, and he proved himself more than worthy of the task, although his appearance caused initial concern. Standing before Brainerd's missionaries was a wilderness hunter with little cultural refinement, but who could speak English. The staff was reluctant to enroll him at all, but finally agreed to do so on a trial basis.

Arch soon became devoted to the Christian faith as well, and ultimately to Brainerd itself, remaining at the mission as a beloved teacher and translator until his untimely death in 1825. Atsi John Arch was buried as he had lived, with much honor, in the Brainerd Cemetery, beside the grave of Dr. Samuel Worcester, who had died at Brainerd on June 7, 1821.

A monument erected by the American Board of Missionaries was placed above Worcester's grave; its inscription was written by Jeremiah Evarts. In 1844, Worcester's remains were removed and reburied in Harmony Grove Cemetery, in Salem, Massachusetts. His monument at Brainerd still stands.

No recounting of Tennessee Cherokee history can be told without emphasizing the influence of one extraordinary Cherokee man and native Tennessean, Sequoyah, or George Gist. Born in the Cherokee town of Tuskegee, and now nationally honored for his eleven years of painstaking labors in compiling the Cherokee syllabus, he first began his quest to put his native tongue into written language around 1809. Although Sequoyah was recognized as a painter and a skillful silversmith, he was middle-aged, spoke no English, read no language and was lame from a hip injury when he began his quest for Cherokee literacy. He was ridiculed for his efforts by all who knew him, and to make matters worse, he had a wife who was inclined to throw away his work whenever she could find it. But these adversities did not impede his determination to better his people.

Sequoyah viewed his tribe's inability to read and write their own language as a severe handicap, of which he saw white people taking full advantage. Observing the power that a written language brought to the white race fired his determination to create one for his own people. At last, in 1821, he announced the completion of his eighty-six-character alphabet, and submitted it to his tribal leaders. It became an overnight success, and all over

Grave of Atsi (John Arch), the rugged young Cherokee whose untimely death, and dedication to Brainerd's students, earned him the honor of a burial beside Dr. Worcester.

Marble obelisk of missionary Dr. Samuel Worcester, who died at Brainerd in 1821.

the nation, within months, Cherokee people were reading and writing in their own tongue, where only a short time before, they had been illiterate.

This achievement prompted Dr. Samuel Worcester to move from Brainerd to New Echota in 1827, to study the Cherokee language. After securing the approval of the Cherokee leadership, he was then able to have type of Sequoyah's alphabet cast in Boston and delivered to New Echota in late 1827. The American Missions Board paid for all printing equipment for the press, but was fully reimbursed by the Cherokee Nation.

In 1827, the *Missionary Herald* printed the entire book of Genesis in Sequoyah's syllabus, and on February 27, 1828, the first edition of the *Cherokee Phoenix* was printed at New Echota. It was an extraordinary bilingual publication in English and Cherokee. This new literacy of the Cherokee people was to become a thorn in the side of whites who could not read or understand the Indian language, but who had been seeking reasons to dispossess the lands they wanted from these "savages." With so many Cherokees becoming fluent in both languages, the whites' arguments of savagery came into serious question.

In reply, when asked what inspired him to devote himself to inventing his syllabus, Sequoyah replied that he had observed that although men learned many things, much of this knowledge was lost for lack of a means to preserve it. In seeing white people with books, he realized that what was written down was not forgotten.

Confidant that his gift to his troubled nation was beginning to bear fruit, and desirous of uniting his splintered tribe, Sequoyah left the Southeast to present his syllabus to the Western division of Cherokees, where it was met with great welcome.

The Cherokee Nation granted him an annual pension of three hundred dollars for life, making Sequoyah the only literary person in America to receive such a monetary reward. The United States government would later honor him by bestowing his name on the giant redwood trees of the West Coast.

While Sequoyah's success and acclaim opened the way for him to become wealthy, this was never his goal, nor did he seek it. He always maintained the old ways and customs, and retained his native religion, his heart ever fixed solely on the survival and ultimate reunification of his people. In this pursuit, Sequoyah perished in Mexico in 1848 while on a journey in search of a reported lost band of Cherokees.

But darker days were yet to come for the Cherokee. On July 26, 1827, the Cherokee Nation, now literate and many in the tribe bilingual, adopted a constitution and Supreme Court similar to that of the United States. But ignoring all moral decency, the state of Georgia passed laws permitting whites to gain possession of Cherokee lands in December 1827. This infamy was enacted at the suggestion of newly elected President Andrew Jackson.

Georgia's new laws declared all the old laws and customs of Indian peoples null and void. Cherokee lands in Georgia were laid out and surveyed, slated to be put up for lottery. These new laws further declared that all white men living on Cherokee property within the state must take an oath of allegiance to it, or be imprisoned at hard labor for at least four years. An effort was then begun to drive the missionaries, who sympathized with the Indians, from Georgia.

Many missionaries removed their families across the state line to Tennessee, which was still within the boundaries of Cherokee land and not subject to the immoral new laws. In Georgia at New Echota, the Georgia Guard arrested Drs. Butler and Worcester, who had firmly refused to take the oath of allegiance, along with several other missionaries. These men were forced at gunpoint to march for miles on foot, and were chained and imprisoned at Camp Gilmer under the most severe conditions. The cost of taking a stand against the persecution of the native peoples was being made unequivocally clear.

When the missionaries' plight was made known, the new Georgia laws were found so offensive that many in Washington opposed them, but to no avail. Chief Justice John Marshall declared these new laws illegal, and confirmed the right of the Cherokee to protection by the United States president from Georgian aggression. In reply, President Jackson merely stated, "Marshall has made his decision, now let him enforce it."

Georgia Governor Gilmer refused to release the prisoners, and on October 22, 1832, the drawing began for possession of Indian lands, which were then swarmed by whites, flooding the land with greed and whiskey. In January 1833, Drs. Butler and Worcester, realizing the futility of their case, withdrew their suit of protest against the state of Georgia and were released from prison. Both returned to Brainerd in 1834.

In 1836, the Treaty of New Echota, signed by Ridge and Boudinot, ceded all remaining Cherokee lands east of the Mississippi to white control, setting the stage for the tragic Trail of Tears. With the Indian Removal now law, the Brainerd Mission closed it doors on August 19, 1838. As recorded in the writings of Dr. Worcester and other records of the times, the Cherokees most emphatically did not ever wish to leave their homeland.

Nevertheless, seventeen thousand Native Americans were collected like cattle and driven into stockades—some to be transported by boats along the river system, others to be marched thousands of miles on horseback and on foot. In the long months that the journey would take, some four thousand

SITE OF BRAINERD MISSION
TO THE
CHEROKEE INDIANS.
ESTABLISHED BY THE AMERICAN
BOARD OF COMMISSIONERS FOR
FOREIGN MISSIONS IN 1817.
FIRST CALLED CHICKAMAUGAH.
CHANGED TO BRAINERD IN 1818.
MAINTAINED WITH AID OF THE
UNITED STATES GOVERNMENT
UNTIL THE REMOVAL OF THE
INDIANS IN 1838.
HERE FORTY BUILDINGS WERE
ERECTED AND HUNDREDS OF
INDIANS WERE CHRISTIANIZED
AND EDUCATED.

ERECTED BY CHICKAMAUGA
CHAPTER DAUGHTERS OF THE
AMERICAN REVOLUTION.
1924

Brainerd Mission's history lies buried in the small, enclosed cemetery, marked by the stone monument placed by the DAR in 1924.

native peoples would perish. The exact number will never be known, as many deaths went undocumented. A number of the Brainerd missionaries, including Drs. Butler and Worcester, accompanied the Cherokees on their forced removal, to begin work anew in the western territories.

The Brainerd Mission property would come into the hands of those who had not labored for it, and with time, its buildings would fall away, its deeds and people left to fade into dim history. Now only the little cemetery is left to serve as a reminder of a time long ago when Tennessee was a thrilling, vast wilderness, and courageous men and women of both the red and white races sacrificed themselves for the good of their fellow man.

AUDUBON ACRES

The Triumph of Robert Sparks Walker

East Brainerd, twelve miles southeast of town.

"Man, separated from nature, becomes a savage." Noted Chattanooga naturalist and writer Robert Sparks Walker, paraphrasing Thoreau, lived his whole life by these words, and urged others to follow his example.

A Tennessee farmer's son, Walker lived most of his eighty-two years in an urban environment. Raised with a large family on his father's Worley (now East Brainerd) farm, young Bob Walker excelled in his studies at the local Walnut Grove School, which he attended while performing the expected family duties of planting and plowing. Although strongly connected to the earth, Walker was drawn more to the charm of nature's beauty, being less enchanted by the harsh drudgery of a farmer's life.

He said in later years that he knew his father often did not know what to make of him, and had even expressed concern that he might never amount to much. But early on, Bob's mother shared with him an appreciation of the land for its beauty alone, and encouraged his dreams of becoming a writer.

Following graduation, Walker spent a few years in adventurous pursuits, peculiar jobs and travel before purchasing, in 1900, a Chattanooga-based agricultural publication, the *Southern Fruit Grower*, with offices on Cherry Street. He remained its editor and publisher for the next nineteen years. After several youthful flirtations, he surrendered his freedom and bachelorhood to wed a friend of his sister Mary, the beautiful Sarah Elberta Clark. This quiet, mysterious, educated daughter of a half-Cherokee Methodist Circuit Rider laid claim to Walker's heart, a claim that would prove stronger than death and last throughout his thirty-six years as a widower.

The two were true soul mates. Raised in the rural countryside of McMinn County, Elberta shared his consuming love of the natural world. They married on August 16, 1904, and after renting several apartments in the Bluff View area, Walker bought his wife's girlhood home on Greenwood

Walker's home at 808 S. Greenwood Avenue, Highland Park, where he lived from 1905 to 1960. Photo circa 1909, after street was graded and limestone walls were built. *Photo by Robert Sparks Walker.*

Avenue in Highland Park from two of her brothers. There, two blocks from the railroad, in an unpretentious two-story frame house on a tiny city lot with an alley behind it, Robert Sparks Walker and his bride set up housekeeping. He would remain there another fifty-five years.

Although on a tight budget, Walker upgraded the house with new mantels and porch columns, Elberta selecting the wallpaper and two slag glass chandeliers. During this time, Walker completed a law degree from Grant University (now the University of Tennessee, Chattanooga), although he never took the bar exam, and never practiced law. By 1909, Elberta had given birth to two sons in their downstairs bedroom at 808 S. Greenwood. Yet despite his city address, Walker's was never an urban mindset. Rather, he and Elberta sought to bring the natural world into their environment. As roads in Highland Park became paved, and automobile traffic heavier, he planted fruit trees—fig, pear, mulberry and a male persimmon that never bore. The three-twigged stick that Walker set out in his front yard in 1908 would eventually grow into a handsome, towering tree. In later years, Walker named his home for this tree, and christened it Triple Tree Tangle.

Walker did not stop at planting trees. He and Elberta took frequent trips to the country, where they gathered wild plants and flowers to bring home for their front, back and side yard gardens. Elberta raised fern beds, canna lilies, daffodils and other cultivated plants, but her favorite garden was a rocky bed of wildflowers, laid out behind the back porch, beside the brick walk leading to the alley. Here she tucked in bluebells, wild asters, spiderwort, daisies and every other wonder she might encounter on a hike with her husband and children. Next to her family, wildflowers were her true love, and best of all, they were free and hardy, growing easily in the city environment.

While Elberta worked her gardens and made hanging baskets of mosses and fern, Walker acknowledged his Tennessee farmer's roots. He plowed "the back forty [feet]" of his tiny yard, and planted small crops of everything ranging from peanuts to Jerusalem artichokes. He also kept chickens, during the 1920s had a milk goat and a pet raccoon some years later for his surviving son that took over their house.

As their boys grew, the Walkers lived up to their name, taking family walks all over downtown Chattanooga, then driving out to the country to hike creeks, fields and woods. Walker's notes from this time reveal that he felt obliged to buy a small farm "for his boys," but he never did this. Instead, he recreated the country in his own yard. He dug a long channel out of the grass, lined it with small creek stones and filled it with water from the garden hose. Here, between this make-believe Lilliputian river and Elberta's deep bank of ferns, his sons and the neighbors' children spent hours sailing paper boats and getting delightfully wet.

Theirs was a perfect family, with an almost perfect life, by Walker's and all other accounts, until tragedy struck in 1915. On returning from a Sunday school event, their eldest son, Robert Jr., was crossing Market Street after purchasing a pack of gum. Suddenly a car driven by a drunk driver swung around the corner. The car struck and dragged the boy half a block before the horrified eyes of his parents and younger brother.

Walker and his wife leapt from their car to collect the child, but his body was crushed and broken beyond saving. In shock, the devastated parents accepted the dubious offer of the drunken man to drive them to the nearby hospital. Cradled in his father's arms, young Robert Jr. traveled to the hospital in the vehicle that took his life. Thirty minutes later, the boy died without regaining consciousness. He had turned eight years old only days before.

Something in Elberta also died that day. Always quiet and retiring, she became withdrawn and reclusive following her son's death. Never strong, her health began a sharp decline as she struggled with the overwhelming horror and grief. After enduring many illnesses, she would die of pernicious anemia nine years later. Walker's account of her passing, written during her final days, is so poignant and filled with pathos that it is difficult to read. She

Walker and his family in 1908. Their happiness was short-lived, but Walker would emerge from his loss to devote himself to nature and his fellow man. *Courtesy of the collection of the Walker family.*

died in the room that had been theirs, he lying beside her, holding her hand, pressing the wedding ring on her finger as she breathed her last.

A man who suffered double tragedies, Walker had every excuse in the book to simply quit and give up. But this was not his nature. While Elberta had fought against the staggering grief until it killed her, Walker surrendered to it, embraced it. Acknowledging that there could be little personal joy for him without his beloved Elberta, he determined that, beyond his one remaining son, his only reason for living was to help others.

The best comfort he received in these dark times was always from nature. Here, he found evidence of resurrection all around, confirming his hopes of ultimate reunion with his lost wife and son. He never succumbed to bitterness, even in times when his own health failed him. He desired to show the Creator's wisdom and reality, revealed in the natural world, and he sought ways to share it.

He wrote articles, columns, books, poetry and, in later years, hosted both a radio and a television show, all to teach and proclaim the wonders of nature. As he continued to serve his fellow man, he received the Boy Scout's prestigious Silver Beaver award for his tireless work among young people, and in 1956, the Chattanooga Kiwanis named him Man of the Year.

But in his own eyes, his greatest achievement was establishing his father's old 120-acre farm on the Chickamauga as a nature preserve in 1948. Known today as Audubon Acres, located in East Brainerd at 900 North Sanctuary Road, it is still open to the public, welcoming young and old to hike its trails, wade the cooling waters of the Chickamauga and take time from the frantic pace of modern life to draw strength and peace from the handiwork of the Creator.

The old farm had been the inheritance of Walker and his five siblings, who were the eldest children of his father and his first wife, who had died of a fever when Walker was eleven. Walker expressed to his brothers and sisters his desire to preserve the old farm, and make it a nature sanctuary. His efforts succeeded—his five siblings sold their shares of the land for a $1,000 apiece—a fraction of its value—and Walker donated his portion.

He was never a wealthy man, but through years of speaking engagements and writings, Walker had acquired a following of influential people who shared his vision. In 1947, he and his supporters founded the Chattanooga Audubon Society, and ultimately purchased the property along the Chickamauga. Among the society's main contributors to the project were E.Y. Chapin and Sarah Key Patten. Mrs. Patten paid for renovations to the fragile eighteenth-century Cherokee cabin in which Walker was born, and the preserve was named the Elise Chapin Wildlife Sanctuary, for E.Y. Chapin's wife, a devoted botanist.

The restored cabin was named Spring Frog Cabin. In the 1930s, Walker had been told by local resident, Mrs. D.F. Ellis (the former Cynthia Warlick, whose grandparents had settled the area in 1834, four years before the Indian Removal), that the structure had been the birthplace of Spring Frog (Tu-an-Tuh), the famous Cherokee naturalist.

She claimed that the description of his birthplace, according to the *Handbook of the American Indians*, which describes it as "near the north

Interior stairs, original restored Spring Frog cabin, 1943. *Courtesy of the collection of the Walker family.*

Fireplace, original restored Spring Frog cabin, 1943. *Courtesy of the collection of the Walker family.*

end of Lookout Mountain, close to the mouth of the Chickamauga," is misleading. Mrs. Ellis said that it should have stated "near the mouth of the west Chickamauga," which empties into the main Chickamauga, a short distance below the sanctuary. Wake Robin Hill, bordering the northwestern and western boundaries of the sanctuary is the nearest point to the north end of Lookout Mountain.

This information continues to be disputed, although there is reason to consider it as viable, given early records of Spring Frog's origins, but the exact truth may never be confirmed. What is known is that Spring Frog was born around 1754, and fought with General Andrew Jackson at the Battle of Horseshoe Bend. He then went west around 1817, joined the Arkansas Cherokees and took part in the Osage war.

Walker's journal records:

> *Amid disputes that the old Cherokee cabin of my birth ought to be torn down, Mrs. Sarah Key Patten, a great fan of historic structures, offered to pay from her own purse for its complete and total restoration. That it will be saved is a great relief to me! It will become our field headquarters, and Mrs. Patten intends to fill it with century-old furnishings, making it seem much like home to me indeed.*
>
> *I have been joyfully occupied laying out trails, about twenty-five now, over the old farm, threading through its most interesting parts. With a hand-operating embossing machine, I am stamping out both common and botanical names of most of the trees. We will have between one and two thousand trees labeled when I am done. To date, I have botanized seven hundred species of wildflowers growing on the place.*
>
> *When Dad [W.T. Walker] bought the farm in 1871 from John and William Ellis for a thousand dollars, there was no well, and he had to carry water up from the creek, get it from a spring two hundred yards away, or else cross the railroad and use a neighbor's well. So he dug a forty-foot well and found a good stream, but poison gas gave them a little trouble until Dad blew out a stone on the bottom, and it burnt up the gas. That old well still gives good water to this day.*

Once the sanctuary opened to the public, Walker traveled to the Chickamauga to hike and teach several times a week. In the old cabin's loft, he kept a trunk of discarded clothes for wading the Chickamauga with visiting eager children and adventurous adults. His creek-wading shoes were an old pair of lace-up oxfords, so dilapidated that their soles had separated halfway back to the heel. Walker often joked that their flapping through the

Cherokee poplar log cabin at Audubon Acres, built circa 1740s. Its original stick and mud chimney was replaced with Graysville brick by Walker's father circa 1880. The cabin was moved and reconstructed in 1970s. *Photo by W.C. Walker.*

water as he walked would protect his toes by keeping away the snapping turtles.

As he grew older, he continued to make pilgrimages to his birthplace to share his knowledge and love of nature with the public, but the better part of his days were devoted to writing at his home on Greenwood Avenue, under the sheltering arms of his triple persimmon tree. There he continued to grow his eccentric crops; keep yellow jacket nests alive in his lawn for study by feeding them melon slices; and cook leg of mutton in a soapstone fireless cooker. He was never too busy for a child, a friend or a dog, and always addressed them with a tip of the hat and a "How do you do, sir." (Yes, dogs too. Especially dogs.)

His front porch became a perfect minefield of jarred insects, diseased tree limbs, leaf clusters and mysterious plant specimens, all left by his readers for identification. Someone brought an odd-looking lizard they had found in a well. Another needed to know what was killing her petunias. He answered them all. If he did not know, he would research until he found the answer. It was his mandate. And all the while he wrote manuscripts, answered

Robert Sparks Walker Jr.,
holding an enormous leaf
from a princess tree shortly
before his death, 1915. *Photo
by Robert S. Walker.*

correspondence and mailed daily stacks of envelopes—working, working,
up until the very day he died.

He had a heart condition for years, but had outlived his heart doctor,
finding that exercise worked better for him than sedentary bed rest, which
was prescribed in those days. Besides walking, favorite forms of exercise were
digging out the basement under his house with a shovel and painting his
home's many porches. He continued to live in the rear downstairs room that
had been his and Elberta's. His friend Claud Fuller, well-known gun enthusiast,
whose collection is today displayed at Chickamauga Military Park, gave him
a handsome secretary desk, but he couldn't work at it, instead keeping an old
Underwood typewriter set up on a table at the foot of his bed.

In 1959, Robert Sparks Walker posed under the Triple Tree persimmon he planted in his front yard in 1908. *Photo by W.C. Walker.*

Robert Sparks Walker at his father's hand-dug well at Audubon Acres, 1951. *Photo by W.C. Walker.*

Granite arrow point marking the grave of Robert Sparks Walker at Audubon Acres, site of his birth and burial. The last line of his epitaph inscribed on the bronze plaque reads: "The mystic veil I may steal through, to walk again these trails with you."

He behaved as a man who couldn't decide whether he was going to live forever or die tomorrow. He seemed driven to complete his journey, to leave no page blank, no lesson untaught, no knowledge unshared. He passed away quietly in his room on September 26, 1960—the same day of the same month that his son Robert had been killed, forty-five years earlier. He left the earth in the same room where both of his sons were born, and where Elberta had died.

His house is gone now, but a few years ago there was still trumpet vine wound around the old triple persimmon, and wild potato vines tangling up the side yard. These lingering traces of his and Elberta's wanderings are remnants of his early efforts to keep his family close to nature, despite urban surroundings. Walker's more substantial efforts to share his philosophy with mankind remain in his writings, and his beloved wildlife preserve, Audubon Acres, which is both his birthplace and burial site. Elberta and Robert Jr. are buried there beside him, a physical testimony of the faith he fortified in nature, which reminds that however long, life is always brief. But after it—reunion.

One of the last poems he wrote was his own epitaph, in which he compares the departing human soul to the butterfly escaping its chrysalis. The last two lines of this poem speak to the visitor to Audubon Acres, from the bronze plaque on the headstone of this native Tennessean who spent all of his eighty-two years in Chattanooga. It reads: "The mystic veil I may steal through, to walk again these trails with you."

Call 423.892.1499 for Audubon Acres information.

CHICKAMAUGA BATTLEFIELD
AND FORT OGLETHORPE

Fort Oglethorpe, Georgia, nine miles south of town.

For all the beauty of Chickamauga Battlefield today, in 1863 it was a bloody, horrific site of death and mayhem, as Confederate and Union soldiers waged ferocious war on each other in the midst of idyllic woods and fields. Many a brave man lay down his life in this place, hallowing the ground with his blood. Most were anonymous young soldiers, known only to their family and friends, but their death no less a tragedy than those well known who perished here.

Chickamauga holds the reputation of being the second bloodiest battle of the Civil War—of the 127,000 men who fought in it, 35,000 were killed or wounded. The 5,200-acre park was officially established on August 19, 1890, when President Benjamin Harrison, a Union veteran, signed the bill opening the way for the land to be purchased and a park created. It would become the first Civil War battlefield ordered preserved by the Federal government. More than a thousand monuments have been placed in the park to honor the many units and states that participated, and to denote their valiant acts and those sites where generals fell.

On the west side of the battlefield, near the location of a pool appropriately named Bloody Pond, is a wood known as Lytle Hill. (This pond now only appears in rainy seasons.) Within its trees stands a cannonball pyramid, marking the spot where Union General William H. Lytle, only thirty-six, commander of the First Brigade in Sheridan's Division, was mortally wounded on September 20, 1863. Twice wounded before, captured and exchanged prior to his fatal assignment at Chickamauga, the courageous Lytle was also a well-known poet. His most popular poem, *Anthony and Cleopatra*, begins with these eerily prophetic lines:

I am dying, Egypt, dying!
Ebbs the crimson life-tide fast,
And the dark Plutonian Hades
Gather on the evening blast…

Lytle's body was discovered by a Confederate surgeon, one of his old brothers in arms from the Mexican War. The good doctor carried the deceased Lytle to his own tent on the battlefield, and buried him beside it. Three weeks after Lytle was killed, his body was removed under a flag of truce by a company of Union soldiers, who were permitted entry for this sole purpose by General Braxton Bragg, Confederate commander. Lytle's body was then taken to Cincinnati, where he was laid to rest at his old home.

Days before the battle, Bragg had removed his forces from Chattanooga to march south, causing Union General Rosecrans to believe the Confederates were headed for Atlanta—a serious misinterpretation. But unknown to Rosecrans, Bragg's forces had obtained reinforcements, and surprised the Union army on September 18 by the Chickamauga Creek, some twelve miles south of Chattanooga.

The First Corps of the Army of Northern Virginia, under Lieutenant General James Longstreet, attached only the day before to Bragg's command, greatly distinguished themselves in leading a Confederate charge that broke through the Northern line, confusing and scattering the Union troops. This strike would earn Longstreet the title "Bull of the Woods" for his role in the battle that sent Rosecrans fleeing to Chattanooga.

Any battlefield is bound to have its tales of ghosts, and Chickamauga is no exception. Over the years, rumors have persisted of uncanny appearances around the site of Bloody Pond, where so many soldiers bathed their wounds that the water turned scarlet. There have been reports of strange, flame-like risings from this water at night, which might be explained as fox fire, or escaping gasses. Less easily explained are sightings of whitish phantoms in the form of swords, flags and crosses. Perhaps they are no more than vivid imagination, but on a site involving so much death, anything could be possible.

When Chickamauga Battlefield was first established as a national shrine, three seventy-foot-high steel towers were constructed at various strategic sites of the battle to accommodate the thousands of Union and Confederate veterans, still living at the time, who came to visit it every year. The last of these towers was removed some eighty years ago, coinciding with the passing of the last remaining Civil War veterans, whose annual pilgrimages honored those who perished, and commemorated their part in our nation's history.

Chickamauga Battlefield and Fort Oglethorpe

Today a portion of the battlefield may be viewed from the handsome eighty-five-foot-high, circular limestone Wilder's Tower, completed in 1904. Built to commemorate Union Colonel John T. Wilder's Lightning Brigade, it was begun in 1892, and paid for by private funds, most of which were donated by Wilder's men.

Today a paved loop approximately seven miles long, intersecting with various strategic smaller roads, makes for easy access to the battle sites. Several of the original homes remain on the battlefield, and have been restored and fixed open so the visitor can view their interiors through grilled doors.

One of these old residences is the Snodgrass House. In May 1927, Chattanooga historian Robert Sparks Walker collected the surviving members of the Poe, Snodgrass, MacDonald and Brotherton families, who had all been living in their homes on Chickamauga Battlefield during the bloody conflict.

Wilder's Tower of hewn limestone, Chickamauga Battlefield, completed in 1904. Much of its construction was paid for by donations from General Wilder's own men.

In 1927, Mrs. Green Reed, the former Julia Snodgrass, seventy-one, was the last surviving member of that family. She was six at the time of Union General Rosecrans's retreat to Chattanooga. The September 18 battle took place across the very hill on which the Snodgrass house stands. Julia Snodgrass Reed said that her first memory was of seeing Union soldiers foraging for food in her father's sweet potato patch. Soldiers would eventually take everything that could be eaten.

But her family did not leave their home until the second day of the battle, when bullets began to fly so thick and fast that some came through the roof. The Snodgrass family retreated to a nearby refugee camp, where they remained for eight days. Mrs. Reed recalled that when they heard a band strike up a Southern air, they realized it was an indication of Confederate success. Being Southern sympathizers, upon hearing it, her family soon forgot its hardships. But it was to be the Confederate's last great victory.

Following Rosecrans's graceless retreat, he was ultimately relieved of his command of the Army of the Cumberland and replaced by General George H. Thomas. Thomas would earn the nickname "the Rock of Chickamauga" for his refusal to leave the battlefield in the face of Longstreet's stunning charge and Rosecrans's abandonment. Thomas was a Virginian who had committed himself to Union service after searching his conscience—a choice that caused him much suffering and considerable personal sacrifice. It is generally accepted that while Thomas's men fought valiantly, it was his example of fearless determination that encouraged his Federal troops to hold the Confederates at bay, thus saving the Union army from a total slaughter.

Larkin Poe, aged ninety-four in 1927, then living at Apison, Tennessee, was also among the elderly residents Walker interviewed. Poe was described as spry, lively and straight of frame, even though he walked with a cane. The white-haired, white-bearded Poe was sharply dressed, and sharp of memory. The section of battlefield known as Poe's Field was part of his old farm, where Poe pointed out many bullet holes and scars on its trees. Poe led Walker and his companions to the site of his former home, no longer standing, where he had lived with his wife and two small children. He had chosen to be a teamster during the battle, to avoid killing humanity, and had come home two days after it was over. He had driven his team from Rome, Georgia, to Jay's Mill, where he then borrowed a horse and rode home by moonlight, the journey made more tedious by the need to avoid the multitudes of dead bodies lying unburied all along the way.

Not far from the Brotherton House, Poe's wife's former home, he ran across a pile of demolished artillery, with many dead men and horses. On reaching Brotherton House, Larkin Poe woke his father-in-law and found that he and others were caring for a number of wounded and dying soldiers on the premises.

Brotherton then rode with Poe to the Poe home site, only to find a pile of ashes where the house had been standing. They found the remains of two dead soldiers in the debris. A desperate search finally located Poe's wife and children at a refugee camp in a hollow northwest of Snodgrass Hill. Some sixty old men, women and children, driven from their homes by the battle, were sleeping under the chilly open sky, and warming themselves by a large log fire, where they were roasting cowpeas picked from a nearby field. Poe had brought back two sacks of corn meal, but wondered how they would cook it without utensils.

Historian Walker and the remaining old residents next went to the Brotherton House. There, William MacDonald, eighty-six, explained that while he had enlisted in the Twenty-sixth Tennessee Infantry, he, too, had been a teamster during the battle, removing wounded from the field and transporting them to Dalton and Ringgold in a flatbed wagon. He said the ground had been so thick with bodies that it was almost impossible to keep his team from running over them. MacDonald's father, John, had been sent by General Wilder to serve as a guide to General Rosecrans, who kept him until after the Battle of Missionary Ridge. A stone tablet marks the MacDonald home site on the battlefield.

MacDonald described the approximate location where his wife and her father had buried seven to nine Union soldiers between the Brotherton House and the road running west to Lytle. This home had belonged to Thomas Brotherton, who had been forced to serve as General Longstreet's guide during the Battle of Chickamauga. In 1927, William MacDonald's wife was the last surviving Brotherton, and although ailing, she had confirmed her husband's account of the burying of Union soldiers in their yard, just north of the house, along a fence row.

She said that her father had dug a deep trench, and she had helped him lower each man into his grave, laying them in a line, end to end. She also described burying one Union soldier, who had begun to smell, "by his lone self" near the refugee camp. With mattock and shovel, she enlarged a hole created by an uprooted tree. She had dragged the dead man over, rolled him in and covered him with earth.

The beauty of the battlefield today belies such dreadful tales of inconceivable hardship and death. We will never really know all the suffering and selfless courage of both soldier and civilian during those dark days, for the terrible, intimate details of such carnage generally go unrecorded. And following the wake of war, few can bear to speak of them.

Members of surviving families of Battle of Chickamauga, interviewed by Robert Sparks Walker in 1927. Left to right: William MacDonald, Larkin H. Poe and Julia Snodgrass Reed, with her grandchild. Picture taken at Snodgrass House, May 2, 1927. *Photo by Robert S. Walker.*

The town of Fort Oglethorpe sits on the boundary of the battlefield. Home to a population of some seven thousand today, it is the outgrowth of the military post that was once located on the battlefield itself. Following congressional legislation that all military parks could be used for army training, Chickamauga Battlefield became a training ground for the Spanish-American War in 1898. It was named Camp Thomas, for General George H. Thomas, the famous Rock of Chickamauga.

Camp Thomas became a temporary home for more than seven thousand regular army infantry, cavalry and artillery units, who were stationed there for a month, between April and May 1898, before embarking via rail for Cuba.

Immediately following their departure came the arrival of the First, Third and Sixth Volunteer Corps, bringing some fifty-eight thousand men and ten to fifteen thousand horses into the camp. The site offered similar terrain and climate to the tropical environment they were due to encounter in the Caribbean, which would accustom the men and horses prior to shipping out to Puerto Rico.

During the rainy season of 1898, some sixty thousand troops stationed there suffered greatly. Men were trapped in mud, their tents pitched in mud and horseflies swarmed everywhere. Troops died with typhoid by the thousands, and it was a most unsanitary situation.

After Camp Thomas closed in August 1898, it was determined that this temporary site on the former battlefield was inadequate for military training, and a permanent post was necessary. In addition, the presence of so many men and horses had taken its toll on the hallowed ground, which could only be rehabilitated with time.

In 1902, the army began construction on a site north of Chickamauga Battlefield that would include officers' quarters, stables, barracks, parade grounds and a hospital. Influenced by architectural style displayed at the 1892 Columbian Exposition, the post was visited by President Theodore Roosevelt in 1903, prior to its completion.

Dedicated on December 27, 1904, the new site was named Fort Oglethorpe, for James Oglethorpe, founder of the initial Georgia colony. It would become home to the Third, Seventh, Tenth, Eleventh and Twelfth Cavalry until World War I, when three camps were added to the battlefield property itself. War games were conducted here, and a young Eisenhower, future president, instructed trench warfare in 1917. Fort Oglethorpe was also one of three camps chosen to house German prisoners of war. At war's end, the temporary structures on the battlefield were taken down.

The Sixth Cavalry, based in Washington, D.C., founded in 1863 by President Lincoln—and with a rich history in Civil War, Indian Wars and Spanish-American War action—was permanently assigned to Fort Oglethorpe in 1919. During the time of peace between the world wars, the cavalry's polo matches, horse tournaments, parades and military reviews drew the interest of the civilian population. During the Great Depression, the post became the headquarters for District C of the Citizen Conservation Corps.

Following the attack on Pearl Harbor, the post swiftly became the site of intensive military training, and the Sixth Cavalry, having replaced horses with mechanized transportation, used the battlefield as testing grounds for its tanks, weapons systems and experimental vehicles. In the desperate cry for scrap metal needed by the nation during World War II for weapons making, pounds of old cannonballs from Chickamauga Battlefield were rounded up and donated to the cause.

When the Sixth Cavalry was transferred to South Carolina in 1942, Fort Oglethorpe housed the Women's Army Corps, and its barracks again became prison to enemy Germans. The WACs remained at the post until July 1945.

But in 1946, the army declared the post surplus property, selling it off to the public; in 1949, the city of Fort Oglethorpe was formally established. Today many of the handsome officers' quarters are private homes, and its former military structures have been turned into businesses. However, much of the post's original flavor is still visible. Its remaining parade grounds, bandstand and Barnhardt Circle serve to remind of the town's proud military history.

Soldiers baking bread, Fort Oglethorpe, circa 1910. *Courtesy of the collection of the Walker family.*

Sixth Cavalry Museum on Barnhardt Circle at Fort Oglethorpe, easily identified by the Cobra Gunship helicopter in its parking lot. Historic homes from the town's military era line the circular street.

The Sixth Cavalry Museum has been established at 6 Barnhardt Circle, easily identified by the Cobra Gunship Helicopter mounted out front. The museum's 6,500 square feet house an exceptional and handsomely displayed collection of military artifacts, uniforms, weapons and photographs, and is open Tuesday–Saturday. Call 706.861.2860 for more information.

ONCE UPON A RIVER

A Race to Preserve the Past

In the 1930s, amid the turmoil of the Great Depression, plans were made to harness the wild and mighty Tennessee River and its tributaries through a series of dams. By 1936, under the auspices of the University of Tennessee's recently formed Department of Anthropology, presided over by Professor T.M.N. Lewis and funded by state and federal agencies, excavation began on Dallas Island in the Tennessee River, north of Chattanooga. This ancient historic site was but one of many slated to be inundated by TVA's construction of its planned Chickamauga Dam.

Work Projects Administration crews were used for labor, and field supervisors hired to oversee the work. One of the archaeological superintendents on this project was Wendell C. Walker, a Chattanooga photographer, cartographer and journalist, the son of Robert Sparks Walker, local historian and naturalist. Wendell Walker was the only native Tennessean on the field staff, and was a meticulous researcher and record keeper, which would repeatedly reinstate him over a seven-year period on many of the joint UT-TVA archaeological river projects. His photographs, and his own original captions that accompany many of them, record the extensive efforts resulting in the discovery and preservation of an ancient people's history, now lost beneath a flood.

Situated twenty miles downstream from the juncture of the Hiwassee River with the Tennessee, and located within the Chickamauga Basin, was Dallas Island, a mile long, dividing the river in two. By the 1930s, the island and river shores had long since become farmland and were owned by the Yarnell and Davis families. Also included in the plan was exploration of the Hixson Mound on the Crawford farm. But long before recorded history, the land had once been an ancient town, situated on both sides of the river at the head of the island. All are now under Chickamauga Lake.

"Typical timekeepers—also expert fishermen. A river catfish which gave its all for WPA." *Caption and photo by W.C. Walker.*

WPA crews expand the trenches at Dallas Island, Yarnell site, May 1936. *Photo by W.C. Walker.*

Once Upon a River

"The excavating crews arrive." *Caption and photo by W.C. Walker.*

As crews excavated, they discovered there had originally been two mounds, later enlarged into one, on which sat a temple. They also found a second ceremonial center on the opposite side of the river, and later a third across the river near the foot of the island. Details of these forgotten peoples' lives began to emerge. Experts at basketry, these old ones had built their structures of horizontal poles, roofed over by slender saplings, intricately woven overhead as a basket, and thatched with grasses. These dome-shaped structures were then lathed with cane and plastered with clay.

Excavations revealed that the Creek ancestors had been skilled craftsmen, who created a range of refined artifacts of stone, shell, metal and clay. Impressed into their pottery were patterns made by fabrics they once wove. Unlike the findings at Hiwassee Island, graves at Dallas were scattered throughout the towns near homes. Some graves were lined with stone, forming a type of coffin.

Skeletal remains showed that the men were of medium stature, powerfully built, with strong features and prominent cheekbones, yet the women were petite, with delicate facial bones and small hands and feet. The ancient bones told that life was brief, barely lasting beyond the forties, with a high rate of infant mortality. Most of their possessions were buried with them, indicating their belief that these articles would be needed on the spirit's long journey to safe harbor in the other world.

In 1938, work began near Dayton, again under the direction of UT's archaeology department, on seven-hundred-acre Hiwassee Island, triangular in shape and located at the confluence of the Hiwassee River with the Tennessee. The enclosed town that once occupied this island dated from AD 1000–1100 to 1700, one of the most extensive records of early Mississippian culture. It was established at the island's head, and ultimately expanded to cover ten acres. Excavations revealed three temples built on a half-acre

Measuring and recording data in the field. Walker with drafting board, 1936. *Photo by W.C. Walker.*

mound some twenty-two feet high. Despite other findings here, no graves were ever discovered on Hiwassee, and it has been speculated that these people may have ceremoniously cremated their dead within their dwellings.

As the continuing work brought forth more information, some team members were led in creative literary directions. William H. Bunce, of the Chickamauga Basin Archaeological Survey staff, was so inspired by his experience that he published *Chula, Son of the Mound Builders* in 1942, a work of historic fiction based on these sites. Later, in 1958, T.M.N. Lewis, together with Madeline Kneberg, documented the archaeological findings of these early river peoples in their classic book, *Tribes That Slumber*.

The dedicated people working on these projects experienced an additional share of excitement beyond the thrill of discovery. As it once was for the Creek ancestors before them, life on the river for the crews and staff was sparse and challenging: camping onsite in tents, sleeping on boats that sank, hauling in food and drinking water, battling insects and reptiles, spoiled supplies and high water.

"The new field camp. Living quarters to left, laboratory tent in center & dining quarters to rights. Left to right in distance; Jane Jennings, Neitzel & Bunce. Walker in foreground." *Caption and photo by W.C. Walker.*

"One of the houseboats, used for living-quarters, sinks in the dead of night—with all hands on board. Close up of the catastrophe." *Caption and photo by W.C. Walker.*

Walker, a former Eagle Scout, reveled in it. He recorded the 1936 and 1938 work along the Tennessee and Hiwassee in his own words, photographs and wry humor, giving us a glimpse of the men and women and mishaps that made up these great river adventures of more than seventy years ago, when a race was run against time to preserve a vital remnant of the ancient past.

Long ago, a Native American spiritual elder, in speaking over the valley towns located along the Tennessee and Little Tennessee Rivers, foretold with tears of a sorrowful time when "the valley would be covered with water and the ancestors would be on the bottom, looking up at the sky through a great wall of glass." With the completed damming of these rivers, this dark prophecy ultimately came to pass.

JOHN DAVID GRAY AND GRAYSVILLE, GEORGIA

Graysville, Georgia, sixteen miles south of town.

Boom towns, just like great civilizations, rise and fall. Some vanish entirely, while others slumber, awaiting an event or an inspired vision to awaken them. Such is Graysville, Georgia, just miles south of Chattanooga.

Established by English entrepreneur John David Gray, it was once the scene of great activity, revolving around the new Western and Atlantic Railroad, and Gray's multiple enterprises.

John D. and his brother William Gray came from England to America in 1818, taking a boat from Boston to South Carolina. The two men, both over six feet tall and three hundred pounds, had been masons in England. But when they became involved with construction of the first railroad built in America—a short stretch of track leading out of Charleston—the brothers soon established a new profession.

Upon completion of the work in South Carolina, the Gray brothers moved to Georgia, where in 1836, they worked on the construction of a new state-owned railroad. In 1848, John Gray's company was one of three to receive a contract to build the stone tunnel for the proposed Western and Atlantic Railroad, which, by 1850, would provide service between Atlanta and Chattanooga, and pass through John D. Gray's north Georgia land holdings on its way.

After Gray surveyed his land near the Tennessee border, where the railroad and Chickamauga Creek pass between two hills, he laid out the town of Graysville. Gray had selected a site with a big spring, an area known as "Pull Tight" by the settlers (for its clay that was sticky when wet). But previously, the Indians had named the place Opelika, and several notable Cherokees once called the area home, including Wulukin and Chief Scrapeshin. The rocky ridge that runs through the town of Graysville is known as Scrapeshin Ridge.

Early photos of the Graysville Mill, rebuilt by the Grays following the Civil War. Today a handsome contemporary home stands on the stone foundation of the mill, which burned again in recent years.

Soon after the town was laid out, a mill was constructed on the south bank of Chickamauga Creek. This was followed by furniture and barrel factories, and a lime kiln. Gray next turned his attention to constructing another railroad line, this one to run from Harrison, Tennessee, via Graysville, to Jacksonville, Alabama. The rail line, however, would never be completed.

By the time the Civil War broke out, Graysville had become a flourishing small town of around four hundred, with a hotel across from its depot. A slaveholder, John Gray used slave labor for his multiple projects, and thus sided with the Confederacy, which would prove his undoing.

From the town bearing their name, the Grays manufactured gunstocks, cedar canteens, buckets and the celebrated Mexican lance for the Confederacy. But Graysville would become the site of several skirmishes prior to the Battle of Chickamauga, only a few miles away, and was fated to suffer the harsh penalties afforded a losing side in war.

With the collapse of the Confederacy, Gray's dreams of an empire perished. His assets were sacked and his labor force was dispersed by emancipation. On November 28, 1863, the mill itself was ordered to be burned down by Union General Sherman, but was later rebuilt by the Grays in 1866. Gray's fine home on the hill above the Chickamauga, overlooking his many endeavors, was also burned, along with his factories, barns and slave quarters.

Two of the limestone footings constructed for his intended railroad to Alabama were ultimately used to anchor the milldam. The mill burned again in recent years, but its limestone foundations survived, and now support a handsome new home, privately owned, but easily viewed from the road. John D. Gray died in Graysville on November 11, 1878, and is buried in the Graysville Cemetery beside a former business partner and fellow Scottish immigrant, Allan Kennedy.

John David Gray and Graysville, Georgia

One of Graysville's remaining historic homes, the Blackford-Gray House on Front Street, is on the National Register of Historic Places. Now a private home, it was once occupied by John Gray's nephew.

The Ward House on Gray Street. Standing on its prominent balcony, victorious Union soldiers assembled to have their picture taken in 1863.

The Big Spring at Graysville, long a destination for summer bathing and picnics, is now overgrown, and sadly much of the town's historic past has faded into the shadows. Exceptions are the Blackford-Gray House, built shortly after the war and once occupied by Gray's nephew. Now on the National Register of Historic Places, it has been restored and still graces Front Street, as does the balconied antebellum Ward House on Gray Street, from which the Union army posed for a photograph. Both homes are now privately owned.

And so a peaceful Graysville slumbers on, patiently awaiting the next John D. Gray to recognize its significance and cause it to bloom again.

BLYTHEWOOD FARMS AND THE HAIR CONRAD CABIN

Cleveland, Tennessee, thirty-one miles north of town.

The sheer beauty of one of the most picturesque farms in southeast Tennessee's Bradley County belies the property's early heartbreaking history. Located near Cleveland, Blythewood Farms's inviting, spring-fed ponds sprout watercress and form little cascading waterfalls that ornament its verdant, grassy, sloping lawns. These create a perfect setting for the handsome, restored Victorian house, its impeccable barns and the outbuildings. This larger home, which is private, was built in 1871 by the Carter family, who owned chenille mills in Dalton, Georgia. Purchased in the 1920s by attorney Pearson Blythe Mayfield, it has ever since been home to his descendants.

Blythewood's owner Bess Neil, who grew up riding horses with her father on the property, married David Neil in 1942. The two undertook the enterprise of starting an American saddle-bred horse farm, naming it in honor of her father. Blythewood Farms is now home to more than a hundred of these handsome animals. Neil and her children still continue the family business of breeding, raising, training and selling horses. The grace of these creatures feeding and frolicking in the lush pastures only adds to the many charms of Blythewood.

An immensely knowledgeable and personable woman, Bess Neil is to be credited with the preservation of her portion of local Native American history. Situated on the hill above her family compound is a well-restored early log house, the history of which, Neil explains, was given to her family years ago by a one-hundred-year-old neighbor, Mrs. Chester Atchley. This elderly woman had been living in the area prior to the Cherokee Removal, and had she not told the following account of the cabin and its builder, priceless history may have been forever lost.

Spring house and the private historic Victorian home at Blythewood Farms. Hair Conrad's original spring meanders through the beautiful property, forming little waterfalls, rivulets and ponds sprouting watercress.

The home was built during 1800–1802 by Hair (also spelled "Hare") Conrad of split and hewn poplar, oak and chestnut logs, some of which are two feet in diameter. The twenty-by-twenty-two-foot downstairs room contains a kitchen and living area, with turned stairs that lead to a generous sleeping loft above. Its log walls are joined at the corners in half-dovetail notches, and its foundation is of native stone. Old records indicate Conrad's property once boasted over 415 peach, 53 apple and 6 cherry trees. The prolific original spring on the hill behind the house still supplies water to the property, forming the beautiful ponds and rivulets that ornament its grounds.

Hair Conrad was born between 1770 and 1780, to Onai, a full-blooded Cherokee woman, and Hamilton Conrad, a half-Scot, half-German immigrant. Hair Conrad's first wife was Katy North, by whom he had three children—James, Betsy and Ollie. After Conrad and his first wife separated, he later married Ollie Candy, daughter of the famous Cherokee Samuel Candy and great-granddaughter of Beloved Woman, Nancy Ward.

It was after this second marriage that Hair Conrad began work on the present log house. In this home, he and Ollie raised their seven children

Blythewood Farms and the Hair Conrad Cabin

The Hair Conrad Cabin, built circa 1800; it was restored by its current owners in the 1970s.

—Elizabeth, Susie, Jefferson, Diana, John, Nancy and Mary. As was the custom of the Cherokees, his children took his first name as their surname.

Conrad became an influential member of the Cherokee National Council, and took part in writing the Cherokee constitution in 1827. He was appointed as one of five delegates in 1834 to represent the Cherokee Nation in Washington, D.C. Conrad's leadership abilities were so impressive that he was asked to serve as mediator on an envoy to Florida, where Seminole Indians were violently opposing U.S. government actions. Letters written at the time by Principal Cherokee Chief John Ross indicate that Conrad and the other Cherokee mediators were never reimbursed for their time and expenses incurred on this peacekeeping mission.

This slight by the government was but a sign of darker things to come, for despite his service to, and standing in, his community, Conrad and his family were destined to become victims of the infamous Removal, and travel the Trail of Tears to the West. Local white residents, who openly acknowledged Conrad as a fine human being, petitioned the government for Conrad and his family to be allowed to remain on their own land. But all such pleas fell on deaf ears. Hair Conrad subsequently led an early detachment of Cherokees

Close-up of cabin's massive logs, showing precision of notched dovetailing in the Hair Conrad Cabin.

to Oklahoma, but his health was badly damaged due to the hardships he had suffered on the journey, and he died on November 2, 1844, near Tahlequah, Oklahoma.

After raising her family, Bess Neil turned her attention to preserving the hewn-log treasure in the woods behind her home. In 1976, she succeeded in having Conrad's cabin placed on the National Register of Historic Places, but this would not provide funding for its preservation. Restoring it to exacting specifications—even finding the required documentation of its once having shuttered windows, to allow the house to be closed up when not open for viewing—Neil paid for its restoration with her own money. Committed to preserving the rich history that is her home, Bess Neil has achieved her goal, and now generously shares it with the public.

Neil tells of the busloads of young Indian people who come from the West to see Conrad's cabin, and immerse themselves for a moment in the

Blythewood Farms and the Hair Conrad Cabin

Interior of Hair Conrad Cabin. Owner Bess Neil has meticulously restored and furnished the cabin with appropriate period antiques. Framed on one wall is an original document detailing Conrad's holdings at time of the 1838 Cherokee Removal.

former life of their ancestors who experienced such tremendous loss in the Removal.

"Sometime they will sit on the front porch," she said, "and take in the beauty of the land with their eyes. They seem to leave changed by it."

Neil pointed out a small remnant of the old Knoxville–Chattanooga highway, on the north side of Conrad's cabin. From its proximity to the house, she stated that it is thought that the cabin may once have been used as a coach stop along the old highway.

Following the Removal, the Cooper family from Texas acquired the property, and remained there for several generations. Their family cemetery is located on top of one of the small, wooded hills behind Conrad's house, and a record of their history has been placed inside the cabin.

For a rare combination of sheer beauty and stirring history, the Hair Conrad Cabin on Blythewood Farms should not be missed. It is open for public viewing on Thursdays only. Call 423.476.8942 for an appointment.

THE TRAIL OF TEARS IN
THE CHATTANOOGA AREA

From Ooltewah, twenty miles northeast of town, to Charleston, forty-four miles north of town.

It is difficult to imagine ourselves stripped of our possessions and forced by law and intimidation to surrender our homes in the land to which we, and our ancestors, have always belonged—a homeland we love dearly and that imparts a great measure of our identity. What would we do?

Most likely we would do what the Cherokee and the other affected southern tribes did in 1838: submit with broken hearts, after having placed our trust in a duplicitous government that considered us no more significant than cattle.

While those Cherokees of the Qualla Boundary in North Carolina (now known as the Eastern Band of Cherokee) were exempt from removal due to an 1819 treaty, those who were living in Snow Bird and the Murphy areas of the state were included in the roundup. The fortunate ones who stayed behind have established themselves in the mountains that have always belonged to the Cherokee people, in the thriving town of Cherokee, where much of their culture and history has been preserved.

However, as history records, the greater part of the Cherokee people, some sixteen thousand of them, were sent west to Indian Territory in Oklahoma. Prior to (and following) the passing of a Federal law enforcing removal, some native people chose to immigrate west on their own. But the more optimistic Cherokees, believing that such an unthinkable thing could never really take place, continued to maintain life as usual on their land. These trusting souls were literally torn from their homes at gunpoint and taken to crowded stockades to await transport to a place that was, at the time, ignorantly considered unfit for white habitation.

Most of these Cherokees were carried by overloaded wagons, or marched on foot the 1,200 miles to Oklahoma; several unfortunate contingencies of them were accompanied by military escort to prevent their slipping away and returning to their homes. The others were taken via river route, enduring hardships through deadly delays as the river levels dropped in sweltering heat. The suffering of the people is recorded in the journal of missionary Daniel Butrick, who accompanied the exiled Indians on the long trek. One of Butrick's entries records the peoples' conditions in the camps as "very much like brute animals—lieing [*sic*] down on the naked ground exposed to the wind and rain like droves of hogs."

While the Cherokee made up the largest contingency of immigrants, Creek, Seminole, Choctaw, Chickasaw and even African slaves belonging to some of the Indians were also forced to remove west. Although the exact number of those who perished on the journey will never be known, due to poor or nonexistent record keeping, it is generally believed that approximately four thousand lost their lives along the trail from exposure, disease and lack of adequate food.

How did this dark chapter in American history take place?

The Cherokee, by the early 1830s, had reluctantly (but pragmatically) recognized the white man's dominion over their land. So they sought to peaceably work in concert with that government's supposed principles, arguing long and hard in the United States court system to protect their rights, but ultimately and sadly, to no avail.

The government's determination to rid the Southern states of native presence was relentless, having the eventual result of dividing the Cherokee Nation into two factions. The larger party, led by John Ross, believed it held sovereign rights to the land, and sought legal assurance to remain there in peace. A second, smaller group, known as the Treaty Party, recognized that the Cherokee cause was hopeless; seeking a peaceable solution, this faction agreed to the government's terms, trading their lands in the South for land of supposedly equal value in Oklahoma.

Major Ridge and Elias Boudinot were leaders of this group, and signed the now-infamous Treaty of New Echota, ceding all remaining southern Cherokee land. While these men may have had good intentions, they did not in any way have the authority to do such a thing. Despite a storm of protest from the Cherokee Nation, the U.S. government readily accepted the bogus treaty as valid, and forged ahead with plans to ethnically cleanse the Southern states of the red race. The treaty had specified May 23, 1838, as the deadline for all voluntary removal of the Cherokee people.

The Trail of Tears in the Chattanooga Area

In 1835, the United States Army established Fort Cass in Charleston, Tennessee, at the Cherokee Agency, which by 1821 had moved to this site in Bradley County from Meigs County following the ceding of the Hiwassee District to the United States in 1819. The agency operated as an embassy, conducting relations between the United States and the Cherokee Nation. It now occupied a site on the south side of the Hiwassee River, and was located near the home of John Ross's brother, Lewis Ross, a wealthy, influential businessman among the Cherokee.

As soon as Congress had ratified the Treaty of New Echota in May 1836, the army began to swell Fort Cass to discourage any insurgency against this treaty, which was considered a highly offensive and illegal document by the people of the Cherokee Nation.

It was hoped by the government that such a strong military presence in the center of the Cherokee's thriving community would prod the people to voluntarily surrender their lands and submissively head west. Fort Cass would eventually occupy roughly forty square miles just south of Charleston, and due to its situation on the Hiwassee River, was to become a main point of departure for the West.

Brigadier General Winfield Scott took command of the Army of the Cherokee Nation in April, 1838, headquartered at Fort Cass. An armed force of seven thousand men drove Cherokees from their homes, which were then plundered and burned, their ancestral farms and lands destined to be won by whites in lotteries. Native people were rounded up from Georgia, North Carolina, Alabama and Tennessee, and by July 25, 1838, nearly seven thousand Cherokee prisoners were confined at Fort Cass, spreading across a section of land four miles wide by twelve miles long. The government had completed its roundup. But Cherokees continued to come in on their own, although a few who were married to whites were given exemption from removal.

By fall of 1838, the land on either side of the road leading into Charleston (now state Highway 11) was dotted with stockades and camps, where some eight thousand to thirteen thousand Cherokee people were held as they awaited cooler weather for deportation. Disease ran rampant in these hot, unsanitary conditions; many perished, and were buried in unmarked graves.

In their final council held at Camp Aquonee, the Cherokee determined to retain their form of government in the new western land. To the very end, Chief John Ross continued to present the tribe's cause in Washington, D.C., but the Removal was not to be averted. Ross returned from the nation's capital to find a white family occupying his own home in Rome, Georgia.

A Senate battle to defeat removal had been led by none other than Tennessee Representative Davy Crockett, who considered the plan odious and immoral. But a reversal of the decision to remove had lost by one vote, and the Indians' fate was sealed. Detachments began to leave for the West almost immediately.

But when reports of disastrous results from the first few government-led detachments filtered back, the Cherokees petitioned for the responsibility of removing themselves. No doubt Cherokee leaders felt they would be more capable and conscientious than the government when it came to protecting the welfare of their people. When John Ross sought approval to take charge of the Cherokee's removal, General Scott, more than happy to have someone else responsible for the mess, gladly turned it over to him.

Ross ultimately oversaw twelve detachments of the Cherokee on their journey west, and all but one of these Cherokee-led detachments traveled without military escort. The last detachment, led by John Bell—which contained a number of Treaty Party sympathizers, who had concerns for their safety among their own people—requested and was granted a military escort.

Cherokee civilians continued to come in from outlying areas to await transport in the hellish internment camps. They would be sent west from eleven separate locations in seventeen detachments, most of them under the direction of various government-approved tribal leaders. Three separate detachments left from Ross's Landing in June 1838.

The last detachment, under the auspices of Federal forces, left in July 1838. A fourth detachment (the first under Cherokee leadership) departed August 23, 1838, from the agency area in Charleston, led by Hair Conrad. But it was held up until October because of low water in the Tennessee River, and illness en route required Conrad to be replaced by Daniel Colston. Three more detachments departed from this location, the final one leaving in December 1838.

A twelfth detachment, consisting of 850 Cherokees and forty-two wagons, left in September 1838, under Cherokee leaders Richard Taylor and James Brown. Brown was a Cherokee planter and Supreme Court judge, and this detachment camped in the fields adjacent to his house. Brown's land adjoined Vann's Plantation on Ooltewah Creek, from which the detachment ultimately departed.

Vann's holdings, which included a large track for horse racing, are today 90 percent beneath the waters of Chickamauga Lake. The James Brown House, built around 1828 of handmade brick, is still standing on a low, sloping hill on Ooltewah-Georgetown Road, about ten miles northeast of Ooltewah. The later addition of a front porch has altered its original appearance, although its handsome brick end chimneys are still visible. Listed on the National Register of Historic Places, it is privately owned and undergoing restoration, but may be viewed from the road.

The remaining detachments set out between September and October of 1838, from Gunstocker Creek, Savannah Branch, Candies Creek, Mouse Creek, Chatata Creek, Ooltewah Creek and Ocod Camp. By 1839, the government's inhumane, imposed removal was complete; the Cherokee and other native presence in east Tennessee and surrounding states was no more.

The People, the *Ani Yunwiya*, had been successfully displaced, but although they had suffered greatly, they were not destroyed. In their new home in Talequah, Oklahoma, the Cherokee Nation would again become a strong nation within a nation, where they would write new history. Still, the hills and mountains of their old homeland remember the ones who left, and call across the miles to many western Cherokee descendants, who make the journey to revisit the land of their ancestors.

While the Cherokee faces have long departed, their influence, names and history remain in these mist-cloaked green hills. On any map of the South, you will find towns and rivers with names like Chattanooga, Ooltewah, Hiwassee, Chickamauga, Ocoee, Toccoa, Resaca and Etowah—ancient native words from an ancient tongue, all with stories of those who gave those names and who once lived there. They have left an indelible footprint in the earth—and yes, the land remembers.

In recent years, interest has continued to grow in preserving the truth of this historic betrayal and appropriately marking the many sites of its unfolding. The Trail of Tears Association was formed in 1993 from the original Trail of Tears Advisory Council. The organization consists of a board made up of representatives from nine states, with its main offices in Little Rock, Arkansas. The association may be reached at 501.666.9032. The following locations figured significantly in the Cherokee Removal.

Blythe's Ferry and the Cherokee Removal Memorial Park

Birchwood, Tennessee, thirty-five miles north of town.

In 1809, a ferry across the Tennessee River was constructed and operated by William Blythe, an Englishman, and his wife Nancy Fields, daughter of

Above: Jolley's Island, and the surrounding wildlife refuge at Blythe's Ferry, viewed across Chickamauga Lake.

Left: The nearly completed Cherokee museum of the Cherokee Removal Memorial Park at Blythe's Ferry. The museum is slated to open this year. *Photos by Gloria Schouggins.*

a prominent Cherokee, Richard Fields. In 1838, Blythe immigrated west with his wife's people. The ferry's location was at the confluence of the Hiwassee and Tennessee Rivers, the northwest boundary of Cherokee land. It would become the last point of departure from their homeland for nine detachments of emigrating Cherokees, numbering approximately nine to ten thousand souls. Once across that river, they were in alien land.

Blythe's Ferry was one of the oldest and longest-running ferries across the Tennessee, operating until 1993, when the Highway 60 bridge was constructed across the river. The Cherokee Removal Memorial Park at Blythe's Ferry is slated to open in late 2008. Its plaza will include a museum housing artifacts and history of the Removal, as well as a meeting room and a Cherokee genealogy room.

The expanse of Chickamauga Lake, a surrounding wildlife refuge and Jolley's Island, which was once home to Cherokee Chief John Jolley, may be viewed from the bluff above the ferry site. Chief Jolley, who strongly influenced a young Sam Houston, left the island in 1818 for Oklahoma, where he served as Principal Chief of the Old Settlers for twenty years.

(The Cherokee Removal Memorial Park is located at 6800 Blythe Ferry Lane in Birchwood, Tennessee, halfway between Dayton and Chattanooga. From I-75, take exit 25 at Cleveland to Highway 60 North. For more information, call 423.334.5859.)

Charleston, Tennessee—Site of Fort Cass

Charleston, Tennessee, forty-four miles north of town.

Although no named town existed during the time Fort Cass occupied its forty-odd acres on the Hiwassee, its site is now part of the town of Charleston. Its major role during the Removal is well hidden today, and all but forgotten by many, but a drive down Market Street reveals a few remaining silent witnesses.

Lewis Ross had operated a trading post and ferry in the area until he was obliged to go west with his family in the Removal. His handsome home still stands at 1 Market Street, although it has undergone several visible incarnations since it was first home to Ross, from 1828 until 1838.

In white hands, his house became the Barrett Hotel, operating from 1838 to 1930, when it was converted into Charleston Manor, a boardinghouse and restaurant. During the 1980s, it became a private home and museum dedicated to Lewis Ross and Cherokee history. Today, it is again a private residence, not open to the public, but may be viewed from the street.

A block down the street, opposite the side of the Lewis Ross House, is the Henegar House, built by Captain H.B. Henegar on the site of the Fort Cass army barracks after the Removal. Captain Henegar accompanied one of the later detachments to Oklahoma, led by Captain Taylor. The house is not open to the public, but is easily seen from the street.

The Charleston United Methodist Church, constructed in recent years, occupies the original site of the Methodist Mission at the Cherokee Agency. Established there in 1825, it was the church in which Lewis Ross and his family attended services.

The Trail of Tears Association continues its work to recover more of the Charleston area's lost history.

The Lewis Ross House in Charleston, Tennessee. Chief John Ross's brother occupied this home until his move west in 1838 with the Cherokee Removal.

The brick Henegar House, built shortly after the 1838 Removal by Captain H.B. Henegar, who accompanied one of the detachments west on the 1838 Trail of Tears. The house was constructed on the site of the former army barracks of Fort Cass.

The Chief John Ross House

Rossville, Georgia, six miles south of town.

The town of Rossville, Georgia, forty-four miles from Charleston, takes its name from the famous Chief of the Cherokee.

John Ross, Principal Chief of the Cherokee prior to the Removal, would retain office upon relocating in Oklahoma, and hold that office longer than any chief in the history of the Cherokee people. Born on October 3, 1790, in Turkey Town, Alabama, to Daniel Ross, a Scots trader, and his wife Molly McDonald Ross, who was one-quarter Cherokee, Ross grew up in the home of his grandparents, located in what is now Rossville, Georgia.

Well educated and a Christian, John Ross found his identity with the Cherokee people of his mother and maternal grandmother, and became a spokesman and leader among them. His eloquent pleas in Washington, D.C., against the Removal are moving and poignant, despite their ineffectiveness against an adamant government. His own family was among one of the last detachments that the wealthy Ross led west by steamboat with 213 aboard. During the journey, his first wife, Elizabeth Brown Henley, known as "Quatie," would succumb to pneumonia in February, 1839. She is buried in Mount Holley Cemetery in Little Rock, Arkansas. A grieving Ross and his children arrived in Oklahoma, where he would be elected Principal Chief of the Cherokee Nation. Ross maintained that office until his death on August 1, 1866, in Washington, D. C., while conducting business for the Cherokee Nation.

The John Ross House in Rossville, Georgia, is the home Ross resided in with his siblings and maternal grandparents following the death of his mother in 1803. Also known as the McDonald House, the restored two-story log home with plank floors and stone chimneys was built in 1797 by Ross's grandfather, John McDonald. The house is situated beside two lakes fed by Poplar Springs, which historically supplied water on this old Indian trading path leading to Augusta, Georgia.

The house contains some original furnishings belonging to Ross and his family, including a handsome dining table and ironstone tableware. The table had been sold at auction in 1834, prior to the Removal. A local white citizen, Wilson Norton, traveled many miles by horse and wagon in a blizzard to purchase the table, and came close to freezing to death to obtain his prize. When the John Ross House opened to the public as an historic property, Norton's heirs donated the table to the project.

Table, ironstone china and woven Cherokee tablemat, original to the John Ross House. The table was purchased at auction in 1834 by Wilson Norton, whose descendants donated it back to the John Ross House when it opened to the public.

The Chief John Ross House in Rossville, Georgia, built in 1797. Ross, Principal Chief of the Cherokee Nation, conducted personal and tribal business from this location. An original spring feeds the three lakes that create an idyllic setting for the historic property.

As an adult, Ross made the house his headquarters for operating a warehouse and trade center in Ross's Landing (Chattanooga), and supervising his large farm. In a long room (no longer standing) that once adjoined the house, Ross presided as Chief of the Cherokees. In 1826, he sold the property and moved to Rome, Georgia, becoming a neighbor of Major Ridge, who was to sign the divisive Treaty of New Echota. Ross maintained his residence at Rome until his removal to Oklahoma. (The Chief John Ross House in Rossville, Georgia, is open for tours. Call 404.866.7404 for information.)

Brown's Ferry Tavern

Tiftonia, six miles west of Chattanooga.

One of the few remaining original structures built by Cherokee hands is Brown's Ferry Tavern, at 703 Brown's Ferry Road, on the south side of the Tennessee River. This large two-story chestnut log house with limestone chimneys is on the National Registry of Historic Places. It was constructed in 1803 by Cherokee leader John Brown, whose extensive 640-acre-farm occupied most of Moccasin Bend. Brown also operated a ferry across the Tennessee River, joining together the Great Trading Path, which is now Brown's Ferry Road. Brown's land marked one boundary of the Cherokee Nation in 1838, and was a stopping point for detachments of Cherokees on the Trail of Tears: the third, Federally led Drane detachment, and the last detachment to leave, led by John Bell.

Although he went west, John Brown returned to live in his tavern in 1840. He died there, and is buried behind it.

Brown's Ferry also has significant Civil War history, figuring in two battles. In 1863, it would become a strategic point in the Union's efforts to reopen the Tennessee River, then under Confederate control. Union Chief Engineer General William Smith and two brigades under General William Hazen and General John Turchin approached by river to establish control of the ferry while General Joseph Hooker and three divisions simultaneously marched through Lookout Valley from the south, toward Brown's Ferry.

On October 27, Hazen's brigade floated downriver on fifty-two pontoons, past Confederate pickets on the side of Lookout Mountain and the riverbanks. Hazen's men secured a position on Moccasin Bend, across from Brown's Ferry, driving back Confederates positioned near the ferry. Union troops formed a bridge of pontoons across the river, allowing Turchin's men to cross.

Brown's Ferry Tavern, built in 1803 by Cherokee leader John Brown, played a role in the 1838 Cherokee Removal. It is located six miles west of Chattanooga, in the area now known as Tiftonia.

Hooker then sent a division to Wauhatchie Station, one of the Louisville and Nashville Railroad stops, to protect communication lines. But Confederate Generals Longstreet and Bragg, observing Union activities in the valley below, mounted an attack on Wauhatchie Station at midnight on October 28.

Hearing the sounds of battle, Hooker, now at Brown's Ferry, sent reinforcements to Wauhatchie Station, causing the Confederates to fall back to Lookout Mountain, and thus giving victory to the Union. Hazen and Turchin's efforts at Brown's Ferry, coupled with the success of Wauhatchie, helped open the road to Confederate-held Chattanooga. The Battles of Brown's Ferry and Wauhatchie signified the Union's first successes in its quest to reclaim the Tennessee River.

A sign in front of Brown's Ferry Tavern identifies it as one of the sites on the federally designated Trail of Tears National Historic Trail. It is also believed that Chief John Ross and his bride Quatie spent their wedding night here. The tavern is now a private residence, but has been meticulously restored and maintained, and may easily be viewed from the road.

THE GRAVE OF NANCY WARD, BELOVED WOMAN OF THE CHEROKEE

Benton, Tennessee, forty-eight miles northwest of town.

Among the Cherokee, women were always afforded a place of respect. At a time in history when white women were considered as household chattel, holding few if any legal rights, in the Cherokee's matriarchal society, women conducted business and possessed the right to inherit property. Children traced their line of descent through the mother. Women were also given the high honor of becoming a *Ghighau*, or Beloved Woman, who would sit in council with the tribal elders.

The most famous Cherokee woman to achieve this status was Nancy (Nanye-hi) Ward. She was born in 1738, in the old Cherokee capital town of Chota, to Tame Doe, sister of the great Chief Attakullakulla, a diplomat and leader who was called "Little Carpenter" by the whites.

Nancy earned recognition among her people at an early age. During the battle of Taliwa against the Creeks in 1755, Nanye-hi, still in her teens, had fought beside her first husband, King Fisher, by whom she had two children. When King Fisher was killed, she picked up his gun and fought like a warrior, spurring the Cherokees to victory and earning the honor of *Ghighau*, a lifetime position generally reserved for women of much more advanced age.

In the late 1750s, she married Bryant Ward, an English trader, by whom she had a daughter, Betsy. Upon taking his name, she became known as Nancy Ward, the name by which history would record her story. Described as a tall, beautiful woman with regal bearing, Nancy is recorded as a member of the Wolf Clan, one of the seven clans of the Cherokee. Nancy spent most of her life in her home village of Chota, located among a cluster of Cherokee towns situated along the Little Tennessee River.

As *Ghighau*, Nancy took part in preparation of the sacred Black Drink, a mixture used in the purification ritual of Cherokee religious ceremonies. More significantly, in her early years with the Cherokee Council, she heard many accounts of the whites' intrusions, their vast numbers and superior weaponry and their insatiable thirst for land. It is possible that her deep desire for peace, for which she is most remembered, became awakened by much of what she witnessed during this time.

If Nancy Ward desired peace with the whites, her cousin, Dragging Canoe, was the antithesis. In one of the councils in which his father, the revered Attakullakulla, expressed a wish to enter into a treaty ceding lands to the whites, an angry Dragging Canoe rose up and declared that ceding land to whites had caused entire Indian nations to disappear. He voiced his determination to fight the white intrusion, and stormed from the Council.

Nancy Ward has been considered both patriot and traitor by those who judge history. On July 8, 1776, she sent word via white traders, warning the Overmountain Men of an impending attack by the Cherokee, which had been spurred by Dragging Canoe's fiery speech. Her reasons are not recorded, but it is plausible that she was seeking to spare lives, both Cherokee and white.

It is generally accepted that Nancy felt her people would benefit from learning many of the white ways, such as raising domestic animals for food, and making clothing. Perhaps she may have seen the future, and the changes it was to bring to the Cherokees, regardless of how valiantly they might fight against it. As a woman and a mother, Nancy Ward clearly valued life, and understood its heavy price.

Following Dragging Canoe's defeat at Long Island, all whites became looked upon as fair game by the disgruntled Cherokee forces. Two unlucky souls who were captured and brought back to the Overhill Towns along the Little Tennessee were Samuel Moore and Mrs. William Bean. Moore met a brutal death in Tuskegee town, while Mrs. Bean was tied up to burn at the stake at Toqua, near Chota.

As the branches around the pole were lit, Nancy Ward—having heard of the intended savagery—intervened, stamped out the fire and released Mrs. Bean. She then addressed the angry crowd of her people, reminding them of her position, and declaring that no woman would suffer such a fate while she was *Ghighau*.

Nancy brought Mrs. Bean to her home in Chota, where she asked the woman to teach her family how to make cheese and butter. She eventually sent Mrs. Bean back to her home with her son Fivekiller and brother Long Fellow as escorts.

The Grave of Nancy Ward, Beloved Woman of the Cherokee

Nancy would again intervene with another warning, this one to John Sevier, of a coming Indian attack, led by those who had joined forces with Dragging Canoe. Yet she was not alone in opposing more bloodshed, being joined in sentiment by many of the older chiefs who also did not support more conflict with the whites.

At the Long Island Treaty Meeting, on July 26, 1781, Nancy Ward unexpectedly rose from the crowd of observers and addressed the group of men who were negotiating: "Women are looked upon as nothing," she stated, "but we are your mothers, you are our sons. Our cry is all for peace." Her words had the desired effect, touching the negotiators, who demanded no land in that treaty.

While Nancy Ward has been called a patriot by some and a traitor by others, her courage cannot be doubted. She had long encouraged her people to turn their attention from warfare to agriculture and stock raising, and she would live to see her influence grow among her people as they adopted more and more of the white man's ways.

At the last council in which she participated, on May 2, 1817, she urged the Cherokee to avoid any more treaties with the whites, and reject all offers to leave their homelands and move west. Due to her health, she did not attend the council in person, but sent her son Five Killer with her message, along with her staff of office.

Womankiller Ford on the Ocoee River, part of the property of Nancy Ward's inn, which she operated from circa 1799 until her death in 1822. A contemporary bridge spans the Ocoee in the distance

Grave of Cherokee Beloved Woman Nancy Ward, and those of her son Five Killer and brother Long Fellow, lie beneath a great cedar tree on the hilltop overlooking her property. Traditional Cherokee prayer flags fly from the cedar branches.

It is thought that by 1799, Nancy Ward and her family had left her beloved Chota to settle on the Ocoee River near present-day Benton, Tennessee. There she successfully operated an inn near her home at Womankiller Ford, a venture that would make her wealthy.

Nancy Ward died in 1822, and is buried on the top of a high hill overlooking the Ocoee River, close to the site of her home and inn. Her brother Long Fellow and son Five Killer are buried in the plot beside her. For a century, the graves remained unmarked, until the fall of 1923, when the Daughters of the American Revolution (DAR) constructed a large pyramid marker of fieldstones over Nancy's grave. A bronze plaque identifies and pays tribute to this remarkable woman.

Nancy's great grandson, "Uncle Jack" Hildebrand, was four years old and present when Nancy died. In his memoirs, and in sworn testimony, he described being in the room when she passed, and reported seeing a light rise from her body, flutter around the room like a bird, then leave through the open door and disappear toward Chota. Others in attendance were also startled by this apparition.

Nancy Ward rests beneath the towering cedar rising from her grave, in the peace she longed for all her tumultuous life. The winding walk up the hill to her grave provides a few moments for meditation on her extraordinary bravery, perseverance and boldness, singular among women of her day. Offerings and brightly colored Cherokee prayer flags left by devoted visitors adorn the overhanging cedar branches and drift above her grave in the winds. We might well imagine that, like Nancy herself, these prayers are all for peace.

BIBLIOGRAPHY

Alderman, Pat. *Nancy Ward, Cherokee Chieftainess and Dragging Canoe, Cherokee-Chickamauga War Chief.* Johnson City, TN: The Overmountain Press, 1978.

Council, Bruce, Honerkamp, Nicholas, and Elizabeth Will. *Industry and Technology in Antebellum Tennessee: The Archaeology of Bluff Furnace.* Knoxville: University of Tennessee Press, 1992.

Effron, Joy Abelson Adams. *Jewish Community of Chattanooga.* Mount Pleasant, SC: Arcadia Publishing, 1999.

Farrar, Rowena Rutherford. *Grace Moore and Her Many Worlds.* East Brunswick, NJ: Cornwall Books, 1982.

The Handwritten Journals of Robert Sparks Walker. Private collection. Chattanooga, Tennessee.

King, Duane, and David Fitzgerald. *The Cherokee Trail of Tears.* Portland, OR: Graphic Arts Books, 2005.

Lewis, T.M.N., and Madeline Kneberg. *Tribes that Slumber.* Knoxville: University of Tennessee Press, 1958.

Magee, David. *Moon Pie: Biography of an Out-of-this-World Snack.* Lookout Mountain, TN: Jefferson Press, 2006.

Moore, Grace. *You're Only Human Once.* Garden City, NY: The Country Life Press, 1944.

Walker, Robert Sparks. *Lookout, the Story of a Mountain.* Chattanooga, TN: George C. Hudson Press, 1941.

———. *Nature Ghost Stories.* Chattanooga, TN: Plantigrade Press, 1998.

———. *Torchlights to the Cherokees.* Johnson City, TN: The Overmountain Press, 1993. Originally published New York: MacMillan Company, 1931.

CPSIA information can be obtained
at www.ICGtesting.com
Printed in the USA
LVHW041302201020
669244LV00007B/339